...it's about time!

by
Nina Warner Lynch

authorHOUSE

AuthorHouse™
1663 Liberty Drive
Bloomington, IN 47403
www.authorhouse.com
Phone: 833-262-8899

Published by AuthorHouse 08/25/2020

ISBN: 978-1-4259-2670-0 (sc)

Print information available on the last page.

This book is printed on acid-free paper.

Wal-Mart™ is owned by Wal-Mart Stores, Inc.
Avon™ is owned by Avon Products, Inc.

TIME and **TIME** again,
My thoughts I've wanted to make known!
"I shall write a book of poetry"—
These thoughts have really grown!

To arrive at a title for this book,
And procrastinating, to me, is a crime!
For most of my life, I've been hesitating,
So, I think now—**It's about TIME!**

About the Front Cover

What do you enjoy doing,
More than anything you ever do?
What seems fulfilling and rewarding?
What brings satisfaction to you?

Well, I shall explain how I chose
The pictures on the front of this book.
Each represents a part of my life,
It didn't matter the TIME it took!

The church I attended, the Missions I supported,
Much prayer had to be prayed,
To make sure of a proper focus,
Exciting, what part each item played!

The dairy produced income,
Amway and Avon helped, too!
Wal-Mart was good in motivating;
So Love Gift, and Mission-giving grew!

God has His way in making sure that
We give what we are able to give,
Our giving to Him is of such value,
And will be as long as we live!

Acknowledgements

TIME for Appreciation and Praise

As I was reading <u>Our Daily Bread</u> this morning, these words prompted me to write this: A person needs three things to be happy—something to do, someone to love, and something to look forward to.

First, I'm very happy when I'm busy.

Secondly, I love my Lord and Savior, Jesus Christ most, because He saved me from my sins and will give me eternal life. *We love, because He first loved us. 1 John 4:19*

Finally, I've looked forward to publishing a book of poetry since I was small. My sister, **Rachel**, has encouraged me to create a little poetry as often as I can, so I have, with her permission, included a poem she wrote in memory of her only child, **Jeff**, who has gone to be with the Lord in 1997. The poem is entitled "Jeff".

Thanks goes to my first husband, **Raymond**, who encouraged and praised me for anything I wrote in the line of poetry. Also to my husband, Max, who helps me to have time set aside to write what I'm thinking. I appreciate **Pastor Gary Colby** and his wife, **Judy**, who have spoken words of "you can do it"! Assistant **Pastor Jim Rairigh** and his wife, **Denise**, have given me hope to get this accomplished ("at any age"). Both ministers have helped me locate the proper scriptures. **Ron** and **Dorothy Martin**, who wrote "Challenging the Road Ahead", are responsible in helping me get this book started. My son, **Greg**, contributed sketches. **Scott Hoffa** has done some sketching in this book. It is my prayer, the Lord will be glorified on each page and I praise Him for the energy and wisdom to complete my first book of poetry. **Mary Lou Lindgren** has helped enormously by proof reading. **Linda Rusie** needs to be commended for make-up in preparing me for the picture on the cover. **Shirley Mutchler** creates hair styles that improve one's attitude—she did that!

All scripture quoted in this book is taken from The Nelson Study Bible, New King James Version.

God's given me another companion
Who's been a great partner and friend!
How can I deserve this one, too—
On whom I can really depend?
(I praise God for you, Max—I love you! Nina)

Contents

A Time for Everything

*In Ecclesiastes 3: 1—11 we find: There is a time for everything, and a
season for every activity under heaven:*

2 *a time to be born and a time to die,*
   a time to plant and a time to uproot,

3 *a time to kill and a time to heal,*
   a time to tear down and a time to build,

4 *a time to weep and a time to laugh,*
   a time to mourn and a time to dance,

5 *a time to scatter stones and a time to gather them,*
   a time to embrace and a time to refrain,

6 *a time to search and a time to give up,*
   a time to keep and a time to throw away,

7 *a time to tear and a time to mend,*
   a time to be silent and a time to speak,

8 *a time to love and a time to hate,*
   a time for war and a time for peace.

9 *What does the author gain from his toil?*

10 *I have seen the burden God has laid on men.*

11 *He has made everything beautiful in its time.*

Section 1.
Poetry of a Lifetime—Family

I'm sharing times that will show to all my readers the value we all place on family life. **Jeff Young**'s life meant so much to **Rachel**, my sister, and she's my encourager in writing poetry. In her honor, I'm sharing in this section, the poem she wrote about Jeff.

God has made everything beautiful in His time.   Ecclesiastes 3:ll

Jeff (August 2, 1951—November 11, 1997)

You have gone on
And left us alone.
Some day, we'll follow, one by one,
To stand before the throne.

Dear **Jeff**, we miss you so,
But God called you to go.
It's hard to give you up this way.
We'll all be with you some glad day.

We wonder why God called you home,
This sinful world, no more to roam.
We're left here, we know not why
That you had to be the one to die.

But really, you are not dead,
For in the Bible we have read,
That you're only away for a while.
We all must walk that last long mile.

Your life was so short and sweet,
Your happy days are hard to beat.
Your happy smile and pleasant way,
Made friends for you every day.

You took many trips with **Ken** and me;
I just wonder why it was to be
That you took this one last ride,
When we could not be by your side.

It's so hard to say good-bye,
When I don't know the reason why.
Some day I will know
Just why you had to go!

Death is so hard to understand,
Until we are guided by God's hand.
May your soul forever rest
In the pasture of the blest!

Love, Mom

Coffing-Warner Marriage

Ray and I were married;
Nineteen fifty-one was the year.
I was just nineteen then—
Our habits, the same—or so near!

Ray had a dairy farm;
I grew up on one, too.—
It wasn't hard to adjust—
Our differences were so few!

We enjoyed four children;
They came at the right time;
Our lifestyle seemed ideal—
There was no time for crime!

As you travel through this book,
You'll notice a family style;
We sought God as our Leader,
As we faced each new trial!

Engagement Announcement

(We now live at 2406 Westside Road Rochester, IN 46975—(574) 224-8131) max.nina@rtcol.com

*(Metea High School Alumni Association Dinner on
May 4, 1996 presented by Nina Coffing Warner, Class of 1948 dedicated to
Max Lynch, Class of 1949)*

I have a story to tell you
About my life since '48.
I was a student at Metea School,
And this fact has guided my fate.

I fell in love with a young man,
Who was in a class below me.
We were the same age, however,
For I skipped grade two, you see.

Our love life halted after graduation
By my father, who was one who knows –
Catholics and Protestants don't mix, he said,
So our relationship came to a close!

So Max went to Ball State University,
I worked in Kresge's dime store.
We each fell in love with another—
Both walked through a new door.

We've had no contact whatsoever,
And everything went fine.
Max and **Kay** had two boys,
Two boys, two girls were **Ray's** and mine.

Max served two years in armed forces,
Taught in Crown Point where he was hired.
Then came back to Gary Schools—
Was principal thirty-nine years and retired.

Ray and I were busy with our four,
Had a farm operation and dairy—
Were blest with countless blessings—
Are those precious memories?—Very!

Then suddenly at age fifty-three,
Ray was taken to be with his Master—
Leaving the family grief-stricken,
Then farm life became a disaster.

My children were such a blessing,
We all hung in there together.
We tried to manage it all,
In the good and bad weather.

Then came the alumni banquet
In '95, the sixth of May.
Max and I met for the first time again,
Since that last high school courting day.

I learned that **Kay** was deceased,
And I knew Max was hurting, too—
No one can know of the pain,
Unless it has happened to you.

So we knew we could be good listeners,
As we each on the other could lean,
Could this be a plan of God,
That we pick up where we were at sixteen?

I want to be sure to mention
As I realize that God is near,
He called **Ben Yantis** to be an encourager
To have Max to attend here last year!

We appreciate **Marge** and **Dan Lynch**;
They deserve a great big tip,
For Max rested many nights there,
Instead of making that ninety mile trip.

All my family have inspired me
To have a happy and fulfilled life.
I'm thankful for their encouragement
As I plan to be Max's wife!

We have enjoyed renewing our acquaintances,
For it's been forty-seven years or so,
We are not the same people now
As we were that many years ago.

I shall love Our Lord as Baptist,
Max will love him with Catholic behavior.
May we show to all this proven fact,
That we look to the same Jesus as Savior!

Now as we look to the future,
There could be little time and health.
It's such a joy for companionship—
In just that, there's great wealth!

Max has asked me to marry him,
I'm as honored as I can be!
There're many widows to choose from,
I'm so glad he chose me!

We announce our engagement tonight,
The wedding is now in view,
We plan to marry in September,
So may we have blessings from you?

Love Poem

We had our wedding rings,
From our marriages we had before.
We thought of no way to divide them
To give to his two and my four.

So we checked with E & E Jewelry
To see what could be done.
This is the suggestion he gave us,
Which pleased each and every one.

The gold was all melted down;
We chose diamonds nearly the same.
We had this made into lapel pins—
A love token they each can claim.

The following verses rolled up as a scroll,
Explains vows they'd want to recall—
It's their's to use as a pin or a pendent,
Truly a touching experience for us all!

Children's Crosses

This cross has a lot of meaning,
For it has been cast for you,
It's love I'm passing on—
This kind of love is not new.

For this gold has been taken
From the wedding rings we wore,
From the day we were married
'Til we could wear them no more.

Each of you children
Can know where it's from;
It's a token of the wedding vows
Of your Dad and Mom.

Nina Warner Lynch and Max Lynch
1997-98

Jim and Kevin

Dairy Farming

Working on a dairy farm,
Is a life I won't forget!
One must be dedicated daily—
It seems like I'm not done yet!
To keep the milking parlor clean,
Was an on-going daily task!
In looking to your milk inspector—
"Is it satisfactory?" you ask!
We were always well blest,
With inspectors who understood—
Always gave me the benefit of the doubt,
More than any inspector should!
The price of milk goes up and down,
It's a gambling of ways and means!
If we keep the parlor up to par,
We've less chance of unpleasant scenes!
Milking, at times, was a joy for me,
For, you see, if I had a grudge,
I had a tendency to take it out on the cows,
And of course, they didn't budge!
At the barn, I did much thinking,
And planning what must be done!
I usually carried a pad and pen,
Noting ideas if I got one!
I give all the credit of successful dairying,
And to get the farm paid for,
(I could never have done it at Wal-Mart—
Not what that job was made for!)
It was to seek the Lord for guidance,
And give the animals good care!
The dog helped a lot, and when TIME to milk,
You just had to be there!

Nancy, you're my firstborn—you've always been a joy!
For, you see, I wanted a girl first,
Instead of a little boy!
You were such a help for me, when **Greg** came along,--
You acted like a mother,
Showing him right from wrong!
You helped with **Leah**, of course,
Being seven years old then,
Hal came seven years later;
You were busier than a mother hen!
You grew up on our dairy farm,
Where everybody had work to do!
You helped in the garden,
And cleaned house and barn, too!
You could scoop cow manure and snow,
As good as any man!
When we asked for your help,
You'd say, "I think I can"!
As you grew older, you had goals;
You were challenged by those around you!
If you came up missing in our busy life,
The basketball court is where we found you!
You enjoyed sports, whatever the season;
Basketball seemed most enjoyable to you!
Your 42-point record remains at Manchester;
(You DID have a good back-up crew)
Since college you did some teaching,
Then on to PHP.
We admire your persistence;
To climb the ladder to be—
Your own boss, which is ideal!
You're a typical woman—you're a gem!
May God touch you in your business—
I know you've close connections with Him!

Nancy, you've been a friend,
When I needed a listening ear!
You seem most attentive
Every passing year!
You really care a lot
As you notice how I'm dressed;
You go to expensive stores
To get me the best!
You've spent lots of money,
That's really hard to make—
Your love is real,
It never seems fake!
You make me proud of you
With your get-up and go—
I think it's not wrong
If I tell you so!
So, as I sit and relax,
Over this cup of tea,
May you be with your best friend—
Soon--I hope it's me! Love, Mom

Train up a child in the way he should go,
and when he is old, he will not depart from it.
Proverbs 22:6

I didn't buy any special cards,
For the network provides none;
So, with pen in hand, I sit and write
An "original" to a special one!

You've been an inspiration, **Nancy**,
For me, in all you do—
You always want the best for me,
And make sure I get it, too!

You don't settle for seconds,
When it comes to my well-being—
I don't just imagine this,
It's what I've been seeing!

My prayer for you this Christmas
Is that God will grant to you,
Peace, happiness, and material possessions,
Enough to give to others, too!

For you're so loving and giving,
That, that which would please you a-plenty,
Would be enough to supply rich gifts
To those who don't have any!

I cherish so much, all the moments
You've shared your good life with me;
I'm looking forward to Christmas
When we can talk, and not work, you see.

I'm thankful for a daughter like you, **Nancy**-
I've been blest that you are my own!
May this Christmas time be a joy for you,
To repay you for the good seed you've sown!

Manchester College Athletic Hall of Fame Induction of Nancy Warner—12/13/97

This is quite an honor
To have as my own,
A daughter who's become famous,
In athletic achievement she's shown!

When **Nancy** was a little girl,
During winter on the farm,
She practiced shooting baskets—
A different way to keep warm.

Along with family and neighbors,
She had cousin competition.
She worked hard to finish chores
To satisfy this great ambition.

Even at grade school at Macy,
During recess or at noon,
She was throwing at the hoop—
Had to stop way too soon.

But her practicing paid off,
She was an asset for the team;
For at Manchester College,
She made true her dream!

Her family was behind her,
And we are to this day!
We are proud of her achievements;
We know God made her this way!

She's a joy to the family,
She's a faithful, caring friend.
She's been a Christlike soul;
One can trust her to the end!

You must understand now,
That these words written here
Are from a very proud mother!—
Yes, to me, she's a dear!

Thanks, Nancy, from Mom—

You've outdone yourself, **Nancy**,
In taking good care of me—
The shower gifts are so delightful;
I'm as happy as I can be.

Body cream, lotion, and bubble bath,
The soap and the towel, as well—
Are all so much fun to enjoy—
Watch me, and you can tell!

The cologne and hose are welcome,
The basket is lovely, too!
I will have an exciting honeymoon,
Much because of you!

You've encouraged me—you've been a blessing,
You've prayed many times for me!
I'm sure I'll be happy with Max—
I think it's God's plan, you see!

I'm thankful for you, **Nancy**;
You make me very proud, too!
I'm blest that you're my daughter—
I'm praying that He'll bless YOU!

Your beauty is something to behold
And I'm not alone when I say,
You have charm, graciousness, and wit—
Many others see you that way!

You are so caring for your mother,
You'll be rewarded greatly some day—
By the One who puts stars in crowns,
And gives honor to those who obey!

I could go on for hours,
With reasons I'm glad you're mine—
Just remember I'm proud of you, **Nanc**,
Please be my Valentine!

Personal Message to Nancy

This message is quite personal,
Yes, it's written just for you!
To express to you what you mean to me
Is what I'd really like to do.

I can think of no better time,
To send these words your way,
For love is the topic of the season,
On every Valentines' Day!

I'll not be a part of the crowd
Of the many who get carried away,
Who send love to cherished loved ones,
Who "buy" cute words to say.

I'm telling you, **Nancy**, believe me,
From the bottom of my heart,
I love you more than I can ever tell—
I just don't know where to start!

I love you for your pure clean mind,
I love you for claiming Jesus your Lord;
I know you follow scripture—
You say it's your fighting sword!

I love you for neatness and tidiness—
I'm sure you didn't get it from me;
But I shall try to get better—
You've been my good example, you see!

This poem was written and your scrapbook was created and assembled for you, **Greg Warner**, as my gift to you---Christmas 2003—by your mother,
Nina Warner Lynch—
12/25/2003

MEMORIES of ME (Greg Warner)

(This is Mom talking)
Greg, this is your life,
From beginning to today!
You were a joy for your mother—
God planned it that way!

Your Dad and I wrote letters,
We were sweethearts from the start!
Here's a couple letters from him,
They're both written from the heart!

*(This is **Greg** talking)*
Here's a switch in the story—
Instead of my birth 'til what's now,
Let's place present-day happenings,
In the front, somehow!

Colorado called for me,
My answer was "yes"!
My! What a challenge—
I must really confess!

Along with other types of hunting,
The most recent is elk and bear!
My goal is to get the trophies,
To show that I've been there!

I was my brother's guide—
He followed really good!
He got his game,
Like a good marksman would!

I enjoy my workshop,
Repairing machinery or making something new!
I make furniture from scratch—
Or, what would you like me to do?

Our Christmas exchange is homemade—
Each gift takes very much thought!
As was our Gift from our Maker,
Then Oh, what a price to be bought!

I really love my horses—
It's characteristic of my Dad!
Some of these animals have been,
The best friends I've ever had!

It's a joy to train them—
It's a major part of me!
I know each one's habits—
They seem like family!

Son **Jeremy** was good help on the farm—
He then went to Purdue!
Why he didn't decide to farm—
I haven't a clue!

It's time to celebrate a birthday, **Jeremy**,
The number is twenty-four!
May the Lord bless you for years to come,
'Til you can't contain anymore!

It's birthday time—
Let's all get in line!
Ride on the pony—
Next turn is mine!

I grew up in 4-H,
The whole family took part!
As **Jeremy** entered 4-H,
Cattle was a good place to start!

Yes, I was in 4-H,
Now here comes my son!
He is showing us all—
Just how it's done!

It takes a lot of work,
(But I hate to admit it!)—
To get to the top! Guess what!
We did it!

My wife, **Jo Ellen**, has worked hard,
Did lots of the feeding!
She's farmed, cooked, worked EMT,
Got me all I was needing!

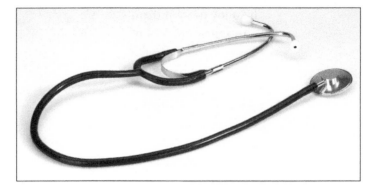

You can tell we enjoy life,
With family and friends.
When we can get together,
Fun never ends!

Amway's been a part of
My life's journey to here!
It's where **Jo** and I made friends,
We shall always hold dear!

We worked, we played,
The memories are many!
Hunger times or real hardships?—
I don't think there were any!

Jeremy was a helper—
How the memories will last!
He worked and played, too,
But he grew up too fast!

We were married in January—
Yes, I took **Jo** for my bride!
Through good times and bad times,
She was right by my side!

If it never happened on the farm,
It never happened at all!
Winters and summers were busy—
As were every spring and fall!

I did some singing—
I enjoy serving in song!
This is one way to witness,
With music, one can't go wrong!

Dairy farming and cattle
Were the income for the Warners!
We worked around obstacles,
And had to cut corners!

To get my basic education,
North Miami was my school!
Reaching for my goals and dreams, however,
Jesus taught me the Golden Rule!

In the Upper Peninsula of Michigan,
Is the hunting cabin at Park Siding!—
If I wrote each story told,
For many months, I'd be writing!

Many years in November,
My Dad brought our Christmas tree!
He cut and hauled it home.
Mom was as happy as she could be!

Jo and I have a veal business;
We hire good help for a reason,
To keep the calves growing,
During the hunting season!

Think of Grandpa and Grandma,
On their way to be wed!
You can be sure as they were moving along,
Interesting words were said!

"May I have some candy?"—
Grandma Warner never said, "No"!
She read me every book!—
She sounded to me like a "pro"!

Greg, this book has many pages,
So as you share it with those you meet,
You'll want to insert more pictures,
To make this book more complete!

To My Daughter Beginning Her Teens

You're just what I need, **Leah**,
To have around the house,
To help wash the dishes,
Or even milk the cows!

Your smile is so precious—
It means a lot to me!
You're my sunshine when it rains—
You're my cup of tea!

So, while you're growing,
As this day does remind me,
I know I can count on you,
For you're right there behind me!

May this, your 'teen birthday
Be one you won't forget!
Out of all twelve birthdays,
May it be the best one yet!

May the Lord bless you
And guide your little feet—
To serving Him more fully,
Cheering those you meet!

I love you! from Mom

LEAH

LOVELY comes forth in my mind,
When I think of **LEAH RAE**!
Her beauty and character are wrapped in one body,
What is a better word to say?

She probably is more ENTHUSIASTIC,
Than all the rest of us together!
Nothing ever gets her down!
She keeps on top, regardless of the weather!

Her **ATTITUDE** is one we all need;
She displays a pleasant one well!
She makes sure she's a good example,
For **Erika** can always tell!

HAPPINESS is what she seems to have,
As she seeks the Lord each day.
This is exactly what **Leah** does—
At times, she'll call and say, "Let's pray!"

Leah, Economical, Artistic, Healthy,
And Resourceful, Are Everywhere in her mode!
This all makes her mother proud!
Heaven bound is definitely her road!

I love you, **Leah**, from Mom

Erika is my little granddaughter,
She was a joy before her birth,
That's hard to figure, so let me explain—
This happening seldom takes place on earth!

You see, **Leah** took me to Indy one night,
And I thought it was to go shopping.
It was before Christmas and I wanted to go;
I was so ready, that there was no stopping!

We were going south and **Leah** slowed down—
She handed me this poem to be read.—
I was hesitant to take it, but listen!—
This is close to what it said!

"Mother, this trip is not to go shopping,
We're going to a specialist for OB's—
You see, I'm going to have a baby,
And you're high on my list to please."

I was just pleased beyond measure—
I had visions of a little girl to enjoy!
I would have been just as excited, though,
If she would have had a little boy!

But, **Erika** has been a delight for me—
She's had beauty and charm all about her!
She shares her love and compliments,
How could I ever live without her?!

She's grown to the age of nine, now,
May be ten by when this goes to press!
I'd like to express my thankfulness,
To a God who answers with a "Yes"!

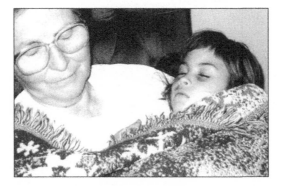

A Day On The Farm

'Twas a warm summer day,
When out on the farm,
Every creature was stirring,
All worked like a charm—

To get all the work done,
Before a down-pour.
There were no people loafing—
Life was never a bore.

The laundry was hung,
All straight on the line
In hopes it would stay there,
And get lots of sunshine.

Dad in his shirt sleeves,
And I in my jeans,
Had just left for the eighty,
To make our ways and means,

When down at the barn,
There came such a noise;
We knew it was created
By one of our boys!

Away to the barnyard,
I flew like a bird,
To ease my anxiety
From the noise I had heard.

The sun was getting higher,
My shadow became shorter,
But my eyes were glued barnward,
As bricks held with mortar,

When what to my amazement,
When I arrived there so fast,
Was that eight year-old lad,
Who was having a blast!

I was scolding wildly,
And he never interrupts—
When I finished, he explained,
"Friskie just had nine pups!"

More rapid than eagles,
She must have given birth,
For we hadn't suspected,
'Twas the last thing on earth!

Hal whistled and shouted,
And out from her nest,
Came that weary mother dog,
But not so, the rest.

For they were too new,
To be up and about;
Since she had so many,
They weren't too stout.

To the top of the porch,
To the top of the wall,
I find myself climbing,
To get away from it all!

And then in a twinkle,
I heard **Raymond** holler,
"What's holding you up, dear,
Each minute's worth a dollar!"

Then I drew his attention
To come look for a minute—
To keep all those animals,
Just knew he'd be "agin" it.

They were dressed all in fur,
There were no two the same,
It would take one whole week
To give each one a name.

I spoke not a word,
But went straight to work,
Filled the corn planter boxes,
Put grease in each zerk!

So we were off to the field
To get some corn planted.
We have a great tendency
To take the elements for granted.

The dark clouds were gathering,
There might be a shower.
It could reach our place
Within the next hour.

The five-sixty sputtered—
Just stubborn as a mule;
I wasn't long discovering,
It was completely out of fuel.

Refueled real quick-like,
While **Raymond** did wait,
But in returning,
A salesman was waiting at the gate!

To white-wash the barn
Was what he would do,
And if we'd only permit him,
He'd make it look new!

Our daughter came running—
I was wanted on the phone;
A neighbor had sows out—
Couldn't put them in alone.

After lunch we had problems;
A water pipe burst.
We called two plumbers—
Used the one who came first!

After all the day's incidents,
I did become worn.—
Do you realize we planted,
Not one grain of corn?

The rain didn't come,
The clothes, they got dry,
But when all these things happen,
We all wonder why.

But we are quite certain,
There's a God who makes sure,
That we have the patience,
For our problems to endure.

We'll plant corn tomorrow,
At least, we shall try,
And take care of obstacles
As each one comes by.

Hal and his puppies
Are the highlight of our cares;
To provide homes for them,
Will be foremost in our prayers.

He sprang to his bed
And on his knees to pray—
(Everyone was all ears,
As to what he would say.)

"Bless all my family,
Bless those who live right!
Bless all those cute puppies,
May they have a good night!"

By Nina Warner--1975

Deer Hunting at the Cabin

The cabin at Park Siding
Is the place the family went,
To leave the farm and rest awhile;
It was always time well spent!

We had many rooms there;
We could spread out and relax.
It was several miles from any town;
It'll take books to tell all the facts!

Fishing in summer and deer hunting in winter
Was the purpose for owning a share!
It was in the center of the Upper Peninsula,
And to see wild animals was rare!

However the bears came at night
To see if we had food to spare!
We soon got on to their pattern;
We left it the last day there!

Floyd Roler was a hunter friend;
He was jolly, he never seemed old!
Then, **Doctor Kahre** owned a cabin next door;
He made furniture, some sights to behold!

Ray found a partner while deer hunting;
Grant Swift was a hunter there, too!
He said, "**Ray,** I sell good insurance!",
Ray said, "I'll buy some from you!"

That sale turned out phenomenal,
For **Ray** was taken in two years.
That amount lifted us out of debt;
It's a dread a widow always fears!

We lost interest to go without **Ray**,
But **Greg** and **Hal** own what we had!
It's still in the family, and a memory;
The kids have fun thoughts of their dad!

Combine Accident

It's hard to find the right words,
And it's something money can't buy;
How do you give enough praise to a neighbor?—
I really don't know, but I'll try!

Bill and **Ora Clemons** have been good neighbors,
They came to our rescue once more.—
A farm accident started it all,
They came again as before.

They came with their own equipment,
They gave their time and gas.—
Thirty acres of corn got shelled,
In less than two hours—first class!

Greg and **Hal** were opening a field
To get **Hal**'s harvest going.
A tree limb caused a sudden halt,
Hal fell into the hopper, not knowing—

The auger was turning and cut **Hal**'s arm!—
He managed to get down and run—
Greg ran to rush him to the emergency room
To repair the damage that was done!

We praise God that it wasn't worse!
We praise God they were working together,
For, on a combine, and alone in a field,
Makes an injury too much to weather!

There's a lesson learned by all of us—
We can't praise God enough,
For taking care of those He loves—
We realize it when going gets rough!

Frank and **Janeal Franklin** were here,
And helped to get this all done!—
Hal's corn is now at the elevator—
Who'd have guessed at the rise of this day's sun?

Thanks to the neighbors from the Warners
Created by Nina Lynch, November, 2000

Mackinac Vacation in 2000

My four children and their families, made
arrangements for Max and me,
To tour and visit Mackinac Island, for our fourth
wedding anniversary!
Correct pronunciation of the Mackinac area, is French
and has no flaw.
Even with a "c" on the end of the word, it's not
Mackinac, it's Mackinaw.
Now this poem is not too organized,--I only write it
when it comes to me!
Each incident is not in sequence—read on, I think
you'll agree!
We left early in the week, so we wouldn't have to
hurry.
We had time to sight-see and shop, and we didn't need
to worry!
The history of Mackinac became very interesting, I
guess, to us.
You'll probably think so, too, that a horse-drawn
carriage was our bus.
There are some facts about the area, I want to share
with you;
Since the Lord has blest us with this joy, it's what He
wants us to do!
As we traveled by horse and carriage, the lady driver
was our informer,
Who gave historical information, while we used
blankets to keep us warmer!
It was cool, but sunny that day, what fun to ride the
carriage horse-drawn!
She explained that 300 horses were used; they're
available at the crack of dawn!

The "Beach House" was a cottage where we stayed two
nights.
We had a waterfront view of many Mackinac historical
sites!
Home-made candy and fudge were 50% of the shops,
Then mementos of the "bridge", was the reason for our
stops!
I was disappointed in over-all shopping, for no
Christlike items could I find.
Toy shops and bookstores were worldly—could only
choose items of that kind.
Food at restaurants were expensive, but we soon
figured out why.
Only by horse, bike, and boat, can support the
demand and supply!
We enjoyed Mackinac Grill at St. Ignace—waitress
Tammy was helpful and sweet!
A vacation is much more enjoyable, when we find a
friendly place to eat!
Kelly gave information as we traveled, steering the
horse-drawn carriage on the isle,
Pointed out the churches—(none Baptist),--told of
interesting history each mile.
There are 500 year around residents—87 are enrolled
in the school.
Grades one through twelve are in the system, have a
football field and a swimming pool.
Interesting to know that last year, two students were
seniors in the fall—
A boy and a girl held their senior prom—competition
was not a problem at all!
At the Traverse Bay Woolen Company, Max bought me
a coat and hat!
All I had to say was, "Let's buy it!"—and generously
Max did that!
The beauty of the Japanese cherry tree, was some
landscaping that took our eye!
Would one grow at 2406?—we might give it a try!
We crossed Mackinac Bridge—hated to come so close

and not do it.
We measured it to be four miles long—I don't think we
ever knew it.
No cars or motorized vehicles!—besides carriages,
bicycles were ridden.
There was a speed limit for bicycles,--any speed over
thirty is forbidden!
Our anniversary was one to remember,--
flowers were a pleasant surprise!
Had safe travel on beautiful highways—fall colors were
a sight for our eyes!
How can we really appreciate, the sacrifice children
will endure?—
To be insistent that parents enjoy life! We praise God
for them, that's for sure!

Created by Nina Lynch
September, 2000

Section 2.
Missions

I'm involved in American Baptist Women's Ministries, so I create time to involve poetry, hoping to enrich the on-going of missions here and around the world.

Walk in wisdom toward them that are outside, redeeming the time.   Colossians 4:5

Women's Day at Crawfordsville Oct 8. 2005
Let's be "born again to be wild about Jesus"
As we give to Love Gift!

This is an exciting time for us,
As we rally 'round this place!
We are dedicated as American Baptist Women,
Seeking Jesus to set the pace!

(Audience please stand)

We've got the spirit!
We know the way!
Let's fight for Jesus!
Let's do it today!

Give me a "W"—("W")
Give me an "I"—("I")
Give me an "L"—("L")
Give me a "D"---("D")
What does that spell?—("WILD")
What does that spell?—("WILD")
Wild about who?---

Give me a "J"—("J")
Give me an "E"—("E")
Give me an "S"—("S")
Give me a "U"—("U")
Give me another "S"—("S")
What does that spell?—("JESUS")
What does that spell?—("JESUS")

WILD about JESUS!

This is the way, we gotta be!—
To get the message, to be set free!

Are we thrilled in this game of life?
To be wild about our Lord?—
To do less than cheering our Captain,
Is what we Christians can't afford!

Let's keep right in there pitchin'!—
Ladies, let's step right up to the plate!—
We can make a home run for our Master—
Let's reach the lost for Him! And not wait!

We are willing to travel the "Red Zone"
On the carpet of His mansion we'll trod!
Our "Global Position by Satellite",
Means one step closer to God!

I think we shall score some points,
If we get on our knees to pray!
His love is explained in Psalm 136
So let's seek Him this Woman's Day!
(Pause)

(Note from Piano—low b natural)

(sing to the tune of the "Notre Dame Victory March")
Cheer, cheer for ABWM
Ring out the echoes—cheering God's name
Send the volley cheer on high,
Shake down the thunder from the sky!
What tho' the odds be great or small,
Our Baptist Women will win over all!
While God's loyal gals are marching!
Onward to victory!

We want a blessing, We want two—
We want a blessing—PDQ!   Yeah!!

Created by Nina Lynch, October 8th, 2005

Circles of Concern

The societies of this association
Were very busy, you will learn,
As I report what was reported to me
Called "Circles of Concern"

It may not seem very much,
To call someone on the phone.
Several groups called shut-ins
And many who were alone.

They prepared TV dinners
For the sick and those who need it.
A visit along with the food is nice.
When we get the call, we should heed it!

The Sangralea Valley Boys' Home
Appeared several times on the list.
Mending was done, clothes were taken.
This recognition shouldn't be missed!

A group sewed kits for the CWS
And sent them to the Middle East.
A rewarding service was this deed,
And valuable, to say the least.

Good used clothing was gathered
Through Church World Service, too.
These were sent to this area of unrest
Across the Mediterranean blue.

The aged of the Neal Home
Were entertained by a few.
The Chase Manor Nursing Home
Had this experience, too.

Knee warmers and lap robes—
Gifts of this nature,
Were taken to these homes—
Were appreciated, I'll wager.

A group took the orphans
On a picnic in the park.
I'll bet this made these kids
As happy as a lark!

They took them on the merry-go-round,
For a couple hours, paid the rent.
Mending was done by the ladies,
And this was time well spent.

Quilt blocks were painted and taken
To people who could really use them.
Try it sometime with your group;
Many places will not refuse them.

The Edna Martin Christian Center
Is a place for busy hands.
Write a note and ask them
To be included in their plans.

Clothing, food, and some groceries
Were taken to the Center.
One group cut out Christmas cards,
And this seemed to be a winner.

One group reported to have
Helped them to their new location.
When a group takes time for this,
Should receive a great ovation!

Bible study groups were started
In a couple different places.
We learn of our commission,
No matter what the race is!

Sunshine boxes were made up
And to a hospital were taken.
These ladies had no idea of the joy,
When they were in the makin'!

A Girls' School in El Salvador
Had postage stamps in their plea.
"As ye have done it for them",
Christ said, "Ye have done it for me".

Trading stamps and BC Coupons,
We gave to this Boarding School,
They can be used for many things,
They can be a very important tool!

Costumes for Christmas programs
Are yearly in demand.
A group reported to have made some.
I think this is just grand!

The folks at the mental hospital
Delight in many things—
Easter hats and jewelry were taken—
My, what joy it brings!

Some groups invited these patients,
Entertained them in their meetings.
I think their hearts were thrilled
To receive such friendly greetings!

You can help a retarded school,
One of these groups did this.
A rewarding experience you'll agree,
One you won't want to miss.

Tray favors, made for hospitals,
Reported some of our ladies.
These are enjoyed by tiny tots,
To people up in their eighties.

One group decided to sit down.
Around a conference table they sat,
And discussed problems right at home—
What do you think of that?

A minister came to another group
And spoke on United Nations.
Through informed sources like this, you see,
We receive a better education.

Being a pink lady in a hospital
Can be done by 'most anyone.
It's not such hard work at all,
And I'll bet it's really fun.

A girl has been sent to Viet Nam
To teach the natives there.
It's a sacrifice this day and age,--
Nearly unheard of anywhere!

Native garments were sewn
And sent across the seas.
Can you imagine how welcome these were?
The folks there are not hard to please.

The Red Cross asks for volunteers,
And some obeyed the call.
They left their work at home undone,
And didn't mind at all.

There was one society reporting
They were blest to the brim of the cup—
Prayed for all, made bandages for the sick—
And I guess that about wraps it up!

We shouldn't get in a hurry
To pat ourselves on the back
There's much yet to do in His kingdom
So many more things that we lack.

By Nina Lynch of the Logansport Association
April, 1998

Sunday Morning Speakers

My friend has come to speak today
Of "Vital Signs", our ABW theme;
An America Baptist woman from Peru—
She knows the structure to extreme!

Barb and **Jim** have the "Poor Farm",
They've sold candy for many years!
May I say they're a "sweet" couple?—
And have no trouble in shifting gears!—

For, **Barb** enjoys Summer Conference,--
Has been on State committees galore.
She's led us in early morning worship,--
How could anyone do more?

So, with pride I introduce **Barb**;
You'll enjoy her as she shares!
She's so mission-minded in her thinking—
For the whole world, I know she cares!
Meet **Barb Poor**!

Ann is a faithful and dedicated person,
She's one of all you American Baptists here!
Her talents are many as she works with people,
For their life and well-being, she holds dear!

She is so excited about her recent endeavor,
As she continues her parish ministry in health.
It's time for her to inform us now
Of her availability—we consider our great wealth!
Here's **Ann Friend**!

ABWM Project
Harghita Christian Camp
Romania

The Logansport Baptist Women
Are co-operating with the State,
To support Harghita Christian Camp in Romania,
Let's give to it now and not wait!

Camping is in full swing
About this time of year.
Let's plan and budget our giving—
It's up to us to make that clear!

Romania is a small country
In Southeast Europe's lower part.
Hungary's on the west, Black Sea—east,
The camp is right near its heart.

It serves nearly 1600 youth—
Unchurched, or with a mental condition.
Learning to sing, worship, and study the Bible,
Taught by Christian leaders, our mission!

They need a chapel and some classrooms,
Crowded conditions make them cry out!
Financial help and extraordinary commitment—
To heed, is what it's all about!

It started in a local American Baptist church,
The First Calvary Baptist church right there.
They have given $50,000 already—
This project is one we shall share!

"One Great Hour of Sharing" funds
Has given a $20,000 grant,
It's a challenge project of World Missions,
And growing seeds is what we shall plant!

The chapel will be $225,000 when finished,
Giving youth and adults more space!
It's to be completed in October, 2000;
It will be done by God's grace!

By project chairman, Nina Lynch

Scholarship Project— Hanna

The Indiana Baptist Women,
Have this project once again—
To support a student in college—
We do this as much as we can!

They'll be attending one of our churches,
And be an active member at least a year.
They must be single—not married,
So their education thrust is quite clear!

As they write up their biography,
How they witness and serve—they explain,
Assuring us that our support to them,
Won't be "money down the drain"!

They will have rated high scholastically.
They will submit letters of reference, too.
There is a deadline to apply for this—
Meeting it is what they must do!

Hanna has met all these requirements!
Her happiness now is a challenge for us!—
We have made a commitment to help her!
We'll give and pray for her!—No fuss!

She'll be given a $500 scholarship,
And there are personal items we'll share—
Our labor of love, we'll be sending
Packages, so she'll know we care!

She's given us some good ideas,
When she completed the personal reference form.
She listed favorite toothpaste, deodorants, and soaps,
All of these she will take to her dorm.

She lists hobby helps and musical interests,
Favorite snacks and small school supplies.
Then there are needs like paper and stamps—
Shopping wisely, we can get good buys!

Hanna will be going to Indiana University,
Then we'll get her college address,
We can send cheerful notes and news items,
Or we can just pray for her joy and success!

So, ladies we have our work cut out for us,
This is a great part of local missions, you see.
We must make sure our young people are supported,
And make the best leaders there ever could be!

"Keeping Balance"

I lost my "balance" at Conference;
I fell and hurt my knee.
Those dear American Baptist Women
Stopped by and lifted me!

I was taken to Johnson Hospital,
And had a few x-rays taken—
Many prayers were sent to the Healer,
But He already had healing in the makin'!

Yes, I had swelling and much pain.
To the hospital **Cynthia** drove my car.
The pain had gone and I felt soooo good—
To find a miracle so great, you'll look far!

The nurse on duty at Conference is **Polly**;
She had come quickly to do her thing!
I can't begin to thank her enough,
So, forever, praises to God I'll sing!

Partner **Sandy** treated me royally, too;
She was insistent that I just relax!
She was thoughtful and wise—
Suggesting I not call Max!

That's an idea so considerate,
For he'd run right down to me!
In the hands of God and 200 Baptist Women,
In what better hands could I be?

Nina Lynch, Secretary, ABWM

ABWM Fall Retreat, 2001

The Peru First Baptist Church
Hosted our ABWM Retreat.
Ruby Taylor was our leader;
She's one who can't be beat!

We sang "Balm Over Gilead",
Led by **Gwen Hardin**, our leader,
And to get the most out of singing,
We most certainly did need her!

We paired off in two's,
We listened, we shared,
Our concentration was "others",
And on our God who cared!

Ruby shared the early years of her life;
She was abused, you might say.
The man she has for a companion now,
Has treated her the very opposite way!

Together, they've been ideal
For us Baptists to claim as our own.
Ruby has been the mostly godly woman
That we have ever known.

The singing of "The Balm of Gilead".
Helped to heal souls that were sick,
If you were slow catching on to it,
Gwen caught you up really quick!

Every comment given was positive;
Nothing came out negative at all!
"Spirit-lifters" were who we became,
Not one person could fall!

"Happiness is like jam", she said,
"You can never spread it around,

Without getting some on yourself",
That's exactly what we found!

"Smile. when you talk on the phone", she said.
"They sense happiness on the end of the line".
If you express disgust or sadness,
They usually have enough without mine!

Prayers are the order of the day—
We could do nothing without it!
If you can't do it effectively, quietly,
Just stand up and shout it!

Stress level was mentioned a lot,
So many have to deal with it, somehow.
Through family, health, or world situations;
We all have to deal with it now!

We never had the same partner twice,
Which got us all mixed up, good!
We made new friends, loved on the old ones,
And hugged them all, if we could!

We all went home with happy hearts,
Determined to cheer up those we can.
It was a day well-spent with other Christians!—
What a joy to be a part of God's plan!

Section 3.
Love Gift

This is the term used for giving to missions in the American Baptist Women's Ministries. Since I've had the chairmanship for this office, I find it more enjoyable to promote it in poetry.

We have known and believed the love God has for us. God is love.
1 John 4:16

Dear Love Gift Chairman,

May the love of Jesus be yours,
As you share your love gift this season!
It's been a joy to show love to others,
We've no doubt that Jesus is the reason!

This parable of the good Samaritan
Is as familiar as the Lord's prayer.
We repeat it many times over
And fail to receive a message there!

I'm going to read it now for you,
Let's try to gain something new.
If we read scripture aloud sometimes,
We hear more what God wants us to.
(Read *Luke 10:25—37*)

When we are challenged with the thought
Of giving our "over and above",
Is our giving from the heart?
Do we really give in love?

Are we acting like the priest
Who had other things on his mind?—
No time for important things,
Or anything of the kind?

Are we like the Levite
Who passed by on the other side?
"What you don't know, doesn't hurt you!"—
Behind this, we tend to hide.

As we consider our Love Gift,
Let's give to those in need—
And be like the good Samaritan,
Answering to those who plead!

If you feel blest tonight,
And feel encouraged where you're seated,
Just share your love gift offering,
The devil will have been defeated!

Just place in this little basket,
As you go out the door.
God will bless you in your giving—
Many times o'er and o'er!
Let us pray

"Mint" to Love

In my Love Gift dedication tonight,
I've used several thoughts, you'll note—
This collection of vases and the flowers as well,
And the fruits of the Spirit I shall promote!

I "mint" to bind this together,
Causing all of you to share
In this ministry of promoting God's love—
HIS giving is beyond compare!

I "mint" to call and thank you,
But my time was in demand.
I "mint" to say, "I love you",
But I knew you'd understand.

I "mint" to send you flowers,
But they cost so much, you know.
I "mint" to pray for you this morning.
But I had some place to go.

I "mint" to say, "forgive me",
But that's so hard to do.
I heard my Lord say, "Bless You, Child",
I hope He "mint" me, too!

Everyone has a collection
Of items they really enjoy.
There are stamps, pictures, and coins,
Spoons, dishes, bottles, or a toy!

There are figurines, dolls, and plates,
Paper weights, salt & pepper shakers, galore,
Mickey mouse birdhouses, and lamps,
And Indian postcards are a few more!

Campbell's kids, watches, toothpick holders,
Mugs, perfume bottles, and cows,
Dollar bills, chimes, and fly swatters,
Some collect these as time allows.

I've recently had my eyes on vases,
Pronounced "vass", according to some,
But vass or vase, whatever the case,
You know where I'm coming from!

The list could go on for a lifetime,
But let's get to the business at hand.
Here are vases displaying gifts of love,
As we share the harvest of the land!

A rose comes to my mind, first;
They express love in so many ways—
At funerals, weddings, to make the sick well—
Just brightens any bad days!

May our giving around the world,
Be accepted to lighten the load
Of those in need of a more lighted way,
Lest we get on the wrong road!

Violets have beauty like no other.
I find joy in watching them bloom.
Let's make a vow of commitment
Before we leave this room!

Its container is the vase of tomorrow—
A joyful noise we'll be making,
As we sing and tell the world,
A love gift offering we are taking!

In the scriptures it's suggested,
We make peace whatever we do.
This vase of pink carnations
Will make us keep that in view.

The world need lots of carnations,
By that, peace would abound!
All thoughts of war would be history—
Not a bomb or gun would be found!

A hydrangea has an appearance of meekness,
Not a bold color clear through.
Though we should be bold in our witness,
To be meek is a godly trait, too!

As His Spirit goes before us,
We should let Him lead the way;
Let's be sure He has our attention
As we give and promote each day!

A lily would suggest kindness—
Even longsuffering, like Jesus portrayed?
If we gave our life for others—
That's the price He paid!

This sacrifice in giving is the greatest
Than anyone has ever done!
This lily reminds us of Easter,
When God sacrificed His Son!

Baby-breath can't be omitted
When you create a bouquet,
A gentleness trait, no less—
It's name just gives it away!

So every breath we take,
We devote it to giving sincerely,
Tenderly, each gift is accepted—
This makes love gift totals climb yearly!

When you see daisies, you smile.
They even look like a smiley face.
Which daisy would show more happiness?—
This one here in this vase!

So, put on a smile, it's contagious,
Practice, put a few on file.
You'll make someone's load lighter,
If they just see a big smile!

The hyacinth shows up early,
Maybe we could dwell on that trait.
When it comes time to send Love Gift,
Let's try not to be late!

Have you had a feeling like this,
That "what I give doesn't count"?
As we pray to send love to others,
The results seem to really mount!

This little petunia is significant,
Although we've heard how the song goes.
He's a lonely little species—Right?—
But he gets our attention as he grows!

We'll not be alone in our giving,
Others will be trying to be matching.
If you glow in this satisfaction,
You'll be setting an example that is catching!

This vase can be used for bittersweet—
Be slow to anger—not upset!
We all have beauty if we look for it,
So please don't give up yet!

Let's not be worthless in giving—
However, pennies really do add up,
And, money given out of tenderness
Causes the over-flowing of our cup!

A chrysanthemum is one we'll display—
How hardy and strong they appear.
They tolerate the colder weather
And perform year after year!

We, likewise, must be strong,
And, too, we're most likely on display
For our fellow servants in the mission field,
Let's perform with giving each day!

Don't you just love my vases?
They each have a story, too.
I "mint" to share each little story,
But that which I've shared must do!

So as we promote love in our giving,
We can be sure of its beauty, too!
We share His gift we enjoy—
Sharing is what we need to do!

Please take a mint with a note attached,
Tonight as you go out the door.
It can be used as needed—
To promote Love Gift is what it's for!

Associational Love Gift Chairman
1998--1999

LOVE GIFT—Spring Conference—1999

The parable of the good Samaritan
Is as familiar as the Lord's prayer.
We repeat it many times over
And fail to receive a message there!

I'm going to read it now for you,
Let's try to gain something new.
If we read scripture aloud sometimes,
We hear more what God wants us to.
(Read *Luke 10:25-37*)

When we are challenged with the thought
Of giving our "over and above",
Is our giving from the heart?
Do we really give in love?

Are we acting like the priest
Who had other things on his mind?—
No time for unimportant things,
Or anything of the kind?

Are we like the Levite,
Who passed by on the other side?
"What you don't know, don't hurt you!"—
Behind this, we tend to hide.

As we consider our Love Gift,
Let's give to those in need—
And be like the good Samaritan,
Answering to those who plead.

If you feel blest tonight,
And feel encouraged where you're at—
Just share your Love Gift offering
From blessings other than that!—

Just place in the handy container,
As you go out the door.
God will bless you in your giving,
In many times o'er and o'er!

Let us pray!

Love Gift Chairman

Offering-----Love Gift

We give a love gift offering now,
It's such a joy to share.
You've showered us with abounding love,
May we give because we care!

We give to camps and Christian Centers,
Even pastoral search and education,
Curriculum and new church development,
Related to financial administration.

Local churches and refugee settlements,
Even ABW ministries, too,
We consider agriculture and World Mission Support—
These are some of what we do!

We pray you'll use this offering, Lord,
As You have always before,
Made saddened hearts much brighter,
As we continue to give more.

May all our partners in missions tonight,
Leave here in persistence to get done,
All the work set for us to accomplish,
So that all the lost will be won!

Love Gift 1998

American Baptist Women's Ministries Conference
Franklin College, Franklin, Indiana
June 7-9, 2002

The Logansport Association of Baptist Women
Was well represented this spring
At the summer conference in Franklin—
We each got to do our own thing.

Some went to workshops on crafts,
Some went to learn how to pray.
Some of us learned more of the structure—
We plan to extend missions this way.

It's rewarding to learn with fellow-Baptists—
We don't always interpret missions the same.
But it's for sure that all our goals are—
To do it all in Jesus' name!

The highlight of the weekend was the missionary—
Who told of many times coping with disaster;
Was athletic director in Southern India;
Helped bring many souls to the Master!

We encourage our young ladies to go,
So that the thrust of missions won't die!
We older ones throw out this challenge—
Come on—take our place—at least try!

P. S. Missionary was **Sandra Schoeninger**

Written by Nina Lynch

[Each blessing <u>underlined</u> should get a
coin put in the **Love Gift Box**.]

I'm your love gift box,
I'm as hungry as I can be,
But please give your tithe,
Before you feed me!
You see, I hold the praises,
Of special blessings of your day;
When you are extra thankful,
And when good things come your way!
Let's walk thru a normal day,
Keeping love in mind—
Put a coin in for thankfulness;
It's amazing what we'll find!
I awake by an <u>alarm clock</u>—
That starts my day.
Put a coin in for that—
A start the right way!
Go right to the bathroom,
And right back of the seat,
My box is there waiting—
<u>Kidneys</u> work—that's neat!
Put the <u>coffee pot</u> on,
My <u>neighbor</u> calls me up,
She says, "I'm comin' over",
"Just pour me a <u>cup</u>!"
Out in the <u>porch-swing</u>,
We chat a little while;
When you get to my age,
It's quite the life-style!
We share exciting thoughts,
We find in "<u>Our Daily Bread</u>",
It's nourishment from the <u>Word</u>.
How much better could we be fed?
I need to run to town
For parts for the <u>plow</u>,
I can't wait 'til later,
I should really go now.

I plugged in the <u>sweeper</u>
In the outlet in the room!
Praise God for the <u>electricity</u>—
Beats pushin' the <u>broom</u>!
Time to get lunch ready—
Let's see, what'll I fix?—
Shall I make it from scratch?
Or use some kind of a <u>mix</u>?
I work away from home—
Some don't—some do—
I'm thankful for <u>Wal-Mart</u>,
I say, "Hello, how are you?"
There's <u>bedding</u> to wash,
There are <u>towels</u> and you name it!
Some count it a blessing—
That's the way I'll claim it!
The <u>sunshine</u> will dry them,
You see, it's real bright;
Hang them on the <u>line</u>—
Save <u>electricity</u>—right?
A call from my <u>grandson</u>—
Please pick me up at <u>school;</u>
I stayed for ball-practice"—
And he calls me—that's cool!!
There's Bible study and prayer
At the <u>church</u> where I go,
I'll pick up my neighbor
Or someone else I know.
Praise God for <u>ministers</u>
Who do well in leading—
They keep me on track,
Which is what I'm needing!
I prepare an evening meal
With things from the <u>freezer</u>.
My! What conveniences,
To make my life easier.

I'll read the <u>daily paper</u>,
Before I "hit the sack".
There'll be plenty to pray for,
As I read front to back!
I'm tired—it's bed-time,
So I praise God for the plan
Of an 8-hour rest time
Made for each woman and man!
Well, I could go on
With blessings to count—
Each day is exciting—
My! How high they mount!
I'm sure you have life—
Different, but just as blest—
Our Love Gift will soar high
To meet world needs of unrest.
Let's put a love gift box
In locations very plain,
So we'll give over-and-above—
Showers of blessing will rain!
They're free for the asking—
Give <u>Valley Forge</u> a call;
Give them your order,
Tell them how many—that's all!
Let's get excited—
That's what we can do—
We can go beyond quota—
To our mission, be true!
God's counting on us,
Let's get our wings unfurled—
In our over-and-above tithing—
Love will conquer the world!

Love Gift

Do you ever take for granted
The things which you enjoy—
From your most expensive possessions,
To the very smallest toy?

I shall make a list of these,
Let's see if we agree,
There're blessings at our fingertips,
But will there always be?

The very air we're breathing
Is free and easy to use,
And now it's being polluted—
Has mankind just "blown a fuse"?

Our homes where we live
Are built so well and strong,
And will not fall down easily,
Until an earthquake comes along.

The beds on which we sleep,
The clothing that we wear—
These all are made available,
Because someone did care!

We ride around in cars,
Maybe not the best,
But it surely beats walking,
You've surely confessed!

The TV and the telephone,
The radio and you name it,
Just sit around everywhere—
All we do is make the payment!

We have books and newspapers
To get all our information.
We take these for granted,
That's my estimation!

We all have a family
Of some sort or other—
If not a sister or brother,
Probably an aunt or mother.

We are thankful for children
Taken for granted a lot;
To the tall and most beautiful
To the tiniest little tot!

There is sunshine and rain,
Which the Master sends down,
Sometimes we smile on it,
But sometimes we frown.

Our church we all know
Is one to be proud.
May we always come and go
And enjoy a big crowd.

Our Sunday School program
Has neat officers in it!
Who wouldn't shirk their duties—
No, not for a minute!

We have law enforcement
In this good land of ours,
(Surely in the promised land,
In their crown, they'll have stars.)

We have a school system—
Maybe some time, we won't.
We say it costs money,
But tell me, what don't?

We have a good minister
Who preaches the Word.
Many times the sermons
Are the best we've heard!

We appreciate our friends
Who stay through thick and thin,
To be unfaithful to them
Would be a terrible sin!

The list is endless
Of gifts from God's hand.
Let's share all this goodness,
We'll be obeying His command!

April, 1998

The Perfect Mother and Love Gift

You are the perfect mother,
In everything you do!
All things are organized and planned,
And happen like you want them to!
You never are late for appointments,
Arriving there on time!
Always balancing your check-book,
And never off a dime!
Your kitchen isn't messy,
For you constantly clean and shine,
So, if an unexpected guest arrives,
You're proud to have them dine!
You make your bed immediately,
As your footprints touch the floor!
You dust and vacuum daily,
Before you ever step out the door!
Your meals are planned ahead of time—
All know when they'll be served!
And, in case of another mouth to feed,
That place has been reserved!
The children's school and sports events,
Are part of a carefully planned day!
You adjust your own activities,
To fit their's, come what may!
You laugh a lot and cry a little,
For nothing upsets your day.
You've been a good prayer warrior—
You let God have His way!
You are sweet to your loved ones—
You never raise your voice.
You settle the major and the minor—
Making the least amount of noise!

You read <u>Our Daily Bread,</u>
You read your Sunday school lesson as well!
You're constantly in tune with your Maker,
There are many ways we can tell!
You give to your Master,
Your ten per cent and more!—
Your Love Gift box is heavy—
You know what it goes for!
I've said all that to say this,
(As if you haven't guessed!)—
You give your gifts to Love Gift,
YOU ARE perfectly blest!

April, 2003

"Love Spreads Where It's Sown"

I'd like to share some thoughts,
Loving thoughts for Mother's Day!
I feel a flow of happiness,
If I show love in some way!

It has been an old, old custom,
To give candy, food, or flowers—
To ones you hold very dear to you,
Ones with whom you could spend hours!

The policy of American Baptist Women's Ministries,
Is to promote love to those we meet!
And, too, we go beyond those,
Not just those across the street!

Our mission goes around the world,
With love, we send money and food!
We satisfy their need with clothing,
That puts us all in such a good mood!

And in our daily living, we're encouraged
To love our fellow man!
It really doesn't take lots of money,
We find instructions in His Great Plan!

We can sow a word of praise today,
Plant a kindness seed,--
Listen to a troubled friend,
Help someone in need!

Compliment a weary soul,
Too fatigued to try,
Shine forth rays of hope on all,
Comfort those who cry!

Scatter seeds of love each day,
Plant each row with care!—
Sprinkle joy along your way,
Soak each one in prayer!

Ask the Lord to bless each one,
And one day you will reap
A harvest full of loving friends,
To cherish and to keep!

As we celebrate Mother's Day,
Let's spread love to all God's own,
For I'm sure you're aware of the pattern,
Love spreads where it is sown!

April, 2005

A Love Gift Promotion

The sun came out brightly—
Dried up the wet lawn!
You just get out the mower,
And the work is soon gone!
GIVE TO LOVE GIFT!

If you've been shopping,
There's change in your purse!
It could get really heavy!—
And what could be worse?
GIVE TO LOVE GIFT!

There was safety as you traveled—
No problem getting there!
You appreciate that blessing!—
The Master surely does care!
GIVE TO LOVE GIFT!

You had a friend very ill,
One in your family got sick!—
With prayer and fasting,
They got well really quick!
GIVE TO LOVE GIFT!

You heard a good sermon—
Pastor stepped on your toes!
We need to be a good listener,
That's just the way it goes!
GIVE TO LOVE GIFT!

You're behind on the dishes!—
What if company comes?
You must clear things in a hurry,
And wipe up all the crumbs!
GIVE TO LOVE GIFT!

A letter comes to you
From a friend of long ago!
It's such a joy to hear
They're well—it's good to know
GIVE TO LOVE GIFT!

There's an ABWM MEETING,
Tomorrow night, by the way—
You have to give the program—
You're free to study one whole day!
GIVE TO LOVE GIFT!

It's nearly time to pay taxes!—
Is there enough money in the bank?
The Lord always provides!—
Yes, He's the one to thank!
GIVE TO LOVE GIFT!

There are many things happening,
How do we keep it straight?
God will be in charge of it all,
If you don't ask Him too late!
GIVE TO LOVE GIFT!

"Love Gift"

God loves a cheerful giver,
So we must strive to give what we can!
We are His instruments He works with,
So let's be helpful in this great plan!

Let's promote Love Gift in our churches,
From the oldest lady to the tiniest boy!
Not only will the gift be a blessing,
But the act of giving brings such joy!

Love from Nina Lynch
Logansport Associational Love Gift Chairman

Love Gift

Halcia Martin is Love Gift for the state!
I called her early today, before it got late!
$16,414.77 is what we have up to now!
#92,000 is a figure we'll reach somehow!
We shall get $7677 in each month ahead
God will help us do it, is what He has said!
I'll send you the figures as she sends them to me!
Prompt to pass the word, is the way we should be!
Don't forget to add to your LG Box
as you count each blessing!
We'll be way past the mark—
that's what I'm guessing!
A basket at the door,
is provided tonight,
If you're planning to give,
and I thought some of you might!

Nina Lynch, Love Gift chairman of the
Logansport Association

Section 4.
Christmas

There are so many ways to celebrate. What a joyous time to use poetry, be it Christ's birth or Santa Claus! Read on!

Glory to God in the highest and on earth peace to men on whom His favor rests. Luke 2:14

The wonderful story of Christmas,
Is enjoyed by many each year.
Expressions of deep consideration,
Are conveyed throughout loud and clear!

The Lord Jesus Christ, our Savior,
Was a gift to all mankind.
To give of ourselves is expected then,
Yes, that's what God had in mind!

The star over Bethlehem signifies
Guidance to someone who's lost.
Could we brighten someone's pathway,
And not ever think of the cost?

The manger of a comfortable stable
Was the place of Jesus' birth!
A birthplace sufficient for leaders of today?—
Never, in all the earth!

The wise men in Biblical times,
In their search for extreme perfection,
Made quite a contribution,
In directing us to a keener selection!

I'm saying that we would be wiser,
If we'd elect godly authority!—
Too many times in government,
The Christlike ones are the minority!

The shepherds are important, too—
They have a message to be told!
They represent the farmers,
Who are worth their weight in gold!

Yes, the shepherds took time from their labor
To rejoice in the celebration!
Let's be following this good example,
Honoring Him throughout the nation!

The inn-keeper has a part in all this—
The city folks come in this class!
The message is real hospitality,
An opportunity we shouldn't pass!

Angels sang out very boldly,
The choir many times is portrayed!
Shouldn't we be so joyous, knowing,
To know Him, we've "got it made"!

Christians all over the world today
Are rejoicing in God's great plan!—
For soon they'll see face to face—
Jesus, the Savior of man!

Christmas Devotional Around the Tree
(Family on Christmas Morning)

We gather around the Christmas tree
On the day of Jesus' birth,
To open the surprise packages,
Not knowing their real worth!

We enjoy the family fellowship,
And enjoy enthusiasm plus!
Do we really stop and think, now,
What God has done for us?

We want to thank you, Father
For the gift that You have sent—
We'll never comprehend it all—
To know exactly what You meant!—

By giving to us so undeservingly
Your only begotten Son;
A sacrifice beyond measure!
Yes, thanks for what You've done!

May we cease to take for granted,
The real meaning of it all!
May we, too, have giving hearts,
And be at your beck and call!

As we enjoy giving and getting,
May our hearts be so in tune
With You, as our guide and leader,
And be ready, if You come soon!

"My Christmas Prayer"

(All players enter to their position at the
same time to the tune of "Away in a Manger".
Rachel, angels, and Mary & Joseph enter
from right of stage, shepherds enter from the left,
wise men enter from the foyer.)

Scripture—Luke 2:1-20—**Jo Kline**
Michael—
The donkey did not mind his load
As Joseph walked and Mary rode
Along the road to Bethlehem,
And God was very close to them!

Rachel—
Sometimes, Lord, the road seems long.
I'm not always very strong.
Any place that I might be,
Please, dear Lord, stay close to me.

Jerry—
There were no rooms left in the town,
So in a stable, crude and brown,
By piles of straw and cattle stall,
God's little Son was born for all.

Rachel—
King of earth and heaven, too.
Earth could find no room for You.
Thank You for that Christmas Day
When you came here anyway.

Carlie—

The darkness in the hills was deep,
As drowsy shepherds watched their sheep.
Then in a blink, the sky burned bright.
The shepherds trembled, sick with fright.

Rachel—

Sometimes I am frightened, too.
Help me, Lord, remember You.
Take away my silly fright.
I am Yours, I'll be all right.

Ashley—

An angel said, "You need not fear.
I bring good news to people here.
In Bethlehem this very morn,
The Savior of the world is born".

Rachel—

Help me hear that news today.
Help me hear the angel say,
"Christ is born for you and me.
Christ is born, and we are free".

Daniel--

The shepherds stood there in a daze,
As hosts of angels sang out praise:
"To God be the glory for this birth,
And peace to all who live on earth".

Rachel—

Angels sang and I will, too,
"Glory, glory, Lord to You!"
Help me sing of Jesus' birth.
Help me work for peace on earth.

Dick—

The shepherds ran to see God's Son
And knelt before Him, every one,
Then ran some more. They had to tell:
"God's Son is born, and all is well!"

Rachel—

Shepherds saw and shepherds told
On that Christmas day of old.
Yes, I know the story well.
Help me, Lord, to gladly tell.
In Your name, I pray. Amen

Erika—

The wise men brought good gifts,
They traveled from afar—
They came to see the new-born King,
They were guided by a star!

Mary Beth—

May the gentle peace of Christmas
Touch you softly from above
As the Christ of Christmas
Fills your home with love!

Robbi—
We travel back to Bethlehem
Remembering Jesus' birth,
But we worship now the risen Christ,
The Lord of Heaven and earth.

Violet--
Christmas is a time of sharing
A time of giving, a time of caring,
A time to celebrate Christ's birth
And wish good will to all on earth!

Mary—
And so our little Lord was born
Into a world all tired and worn.
He came so sin and death might end.
He came to make us each God's friend.

Children sing—"Away in a Manger"
Soloists—**Erika and Michael**

Solo—**Michael Milroy**

Children sing—"Joy, Joy, Joy to the World"

All leave stage going out to the same direction they came in.

The Christmas Candy Cane

The Christmas candy cane
Has a story so unique!
Should it happen to come to life,
'Twould have exciting words to speak!

You see, it was created
By a Hoosier of great worth,
Who explains the life of Jesus—
Of His ministry, death, and birth.

The white symbolizes purity—
In Him there was no sin.
The candy is hard—the Solid Rock,
Firmness shows His faithfulness to men.

It's the form of a "J", who is Jesus,
Our Savior to earth He came!
It's a perfect staff for a shepherd,
Reaching His sheep, as He calls us by name!

The red stripes remind us of scourging,
Which are the ones by which we are healed;
One stripe tells of blood shed by Christ,
Our redemption then became sealed!

The candy cane has a meaning at Christmas
It's a meaning we all need to hear.
Remember the wonder of Jesus and His love,
Let's proclaim it loud and clear!

Night Before Christmas

(I was an Avon representative)

'Twas the week before Christmas,
It was fast to arrive,
I must go out to deliver
All of Campaign twenty-five!

The orders were all sacked,
With a gift in each one,
Hoping each customer
Would appreciate what I'd done!

School kids will be home
On their Christmas vacation,
And I might reveal secrets,
So each stop means hesitation!

So I get all dressed up—
Ready to make all my stops!
I must really go fast,
Hoping not to see cops!—

When out in the garage,
As I was starting to go,
I noticed my car
Had a flat tire!—Oh, no!

Away to the telephone
I flew to make a call
To get help to fix it,
Or change it—that's all!

The sun was peeking out
From clouds suggesting snow!
It made me button my coat,
Preparing for the wind to blow!

Then I began wondering
If my "Feelin' Fresh" was working,
For I had "New Vitality",
And I'd hear people smirking!

My "skin was so soft"—
I was good advertisement!
Avon has taught me
What good advice meant!

More rapid than eagles,
That man fixed my flat!
I gave him some "rugger"
For I appreciated that!

To the top of the porch,
And to each customer's front door,
I delivered each order,
And even tried to sell more!

And I heard in a twinkle,
I heard a customer say.
"Do you happen to have with you
Any extra Avon today?"

Judy Duncan, my manager,
Has made a clear stand,
That it's wise to have
Extra Avon on hand!

So quickly I sold her
Pavielle with delight,
For she needed an exchange gift
For a party that night!

I spoke not a word,
Besides Merry Christmas, you see,
For customer after customer
Was waiting on me.

I sprang through my day,
Got all deliveries made;
Customers were really happy—
It's because I had prayed!

I asked God to touch
Each home on my route,
And let each of them know
What Christmas is about!

If I can make people happy
With a product so great,
I can witness more efficiently
For the One whose birth we celebrate!

Christmas—1983

Is Santa Saved?

I'd been doing a lot of thinking
About a year ago or so;
Are these thoughts common to others?
I'll probably never know.

I'm about to give you, word for word,
These thoughts that puzzled my head.
In my prayer to God about it,
This is what I said—

When Santa comes on Christmas,
I know what I will do,
I'll ask him if he knows Jesus,
I think he should, don't you?

He'd be a terrific witness
To get the Word to all,
Going house to house on Christmas eve,
Or when he goes to the shopping mall.

He's one who attracts attention,
Which is hard for some of us—
I know Santa could win some souls
Without hardly making a fuss.

How can I approach him?—
I am always asleep when he comes!
I leave him milk and a sandwich,
And all that's left is the crumbs.

How about leaving him a note,
And put it in really plain sight,
So he'd be sure to get the message
On that busy delivery night?

So I placed an open Bible
On the table with his snack,
And put a note in really big letters—
He'd see it before opening his pack!

I marked John 3:16
For him to read the very first thing,
He could play my tape player—
The song—"I'm the Child of the King".

I wrote these words on a paper,
Left an extra paper and pen,
And told him I really loved Jesus,
For He will take away my sin.

And on this note I asked him,
If he knew Jesus, my Lord,
And that I would share my Bible,
I've been taught it's a great sword.

Well, as before, I didn't hear him,
But I hurried to find his tracks.
Sure enough, he'd been there,
I'm excited to share the facts!

His note that he left, said this,
(Now can't you hear him say?)
"Ho, ho, ho, my dear friend,
You've been really faithful to pray!

Yes, I am a part of the plan,
God has honored me with this flight,
Spreading peace and goodwill everywhere,
But it's hard to get it done in one night.

So, why don't you try to help me,
And continue to share the good news,
That Jesus was born to save the lost,
Not a soul would He want to lose."

So I praise the Lord for Santa,
I can depend on what he said,
I shall pray for persistence to witness,
Each night when I go to bed!

Composed--1998

December Twenty-sixth

'Twas the day after Christmas,
When all through the house,
Not a creature was stirring,
Not even a mouse!

The stockings were dumped out
On the living room floor—
The children had eaten—
Couldn't hold anymore.

Mama had her dust rag,
I ran the sweeper;
The big stack of trash
Couldn't get any deeper—

When out in the breezeway
There 'rose such a clatter,
I unplugged my sweeper,
To see what was the matter!

Away to the breezeway,
I flew in a rage—
I sounded like a lion,
Who'd gotten out of his cage—

When what to my wondering
Eyes should appear,
But two hungry dogs,
And four cats that looked queer!

As I drew myself backward,
And about to shut the door,
I suddenly realized
What they were there for.

They <u>weren't</u> chubby and plump,
They were scrawny little critters—
The fact they hadn't eaten,
Just gave me the jitters!

I spoke not a word
But went for some food,
They were nearly starved,
And I couldn't be rude.

They barked and they mewed
In appreciation I know—
My heart was warmed—
You could tell it so!—

For I didn't mind the cleaning—
That must be done right—
I'll be thankful for animals
In my prayers tonight!
1996

"Gifts For Jesus"—

(There will be three people to play the parts
of Joseph, Mary, and Baby Jesus.)
"Silent Night" will be played on the piano as the cast comes in to take
their place. Someone will read Matthew 2:1,2. All who have something
for Jesus will come to the manger one at a time and speak their recitation
and present their gift. All will sing "Go Tell it on the Mountain". All
will get in their places to enjoy the rest of the worship service, while the
pianist plays "Silent Night" again.

The STAR of Bethlehem is our guide.
It guided the wise men from afar.
It makes everything bright at night—
It shows us just where we are!

I have a gift for Jesus—
I know He'll like it well;
He'll have lots of fun with it—
It's a merry Christmas BELL!

An ANGEL for the top of the tree,
Is what I've brought to share.
The angel brought good news, you know—
News, only angels can bear!

The BIBLE is a part of Christmas.
Here, the story is told very clearly—
How Jesus was born in a manger—
It tells it all very dearly!

I brought a TOY for Jesus,
He will soon be ready to play.
I want Him to have it!—
He'll think it's just O. K. !

A CROWN is for a King—
That's what Jesus came to be!—
To rule over hearts of man.
I want Him to be King for me!

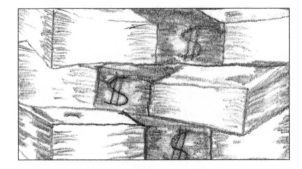

Jesus can't spend MONEY,
But He'll tell me how I can,
So I can help feed the hungry—
Either here, or in some other land!

I have something for my Savior—
It's all wrapped up so neat!
I want Jesus to enjoy it—
For it's something good to EAT!

The BLANKET is to keep me warm!
Do you think Jesus could use it, too?
There are lots who suffer the cold!—
To share it is what I'd like to do!

I've brought a SMILE for Jesus;
I'm practicing on it today!
It's a sign to show Him I'm happy!—
He promised to take my sins away!

Here is a CUP OF COLD WATER,
Sometimes it's a welcome sight!
May we always keep one ready,
For it's a blessing day or night!

Section 5.
Palm Sunday and Easter

Time to go and tell others!

He is not here; He is risen as He said.
Matthew 28:6

Palms

(tune to "Jesus Loves Me")

Let us wave our palms up high,
As the King comes passing by.
Little ones can wave them, too.
Praising Him is what they do!

Yes, Jesus loves me,
Yes, Jesus loves me,
Yes, Jesus loves me,

The Bible tells me so!

The PALMS were laid before Him,

As Jesus rode into town.
It was a way to honor a King—
That's why they laid them down.
I'm holding the long NAILS
Used to put Jesus on the "tree"—
They couldn't hold the Master,
He came down just for me!
I have my BIBLE that tells
The greatest story, ever!
It says Jesus lives today,
And He will leave us?—Never!
The STONE before the tomb,
Couldn't be moved by any man,
But our Father has the power
To carry out His plan!
I have an empty CROSS—
They had hung Jesus here!
But He is risen from the dead,
So, now we have no fear!
The ANGELS had a part
Of sharing the good news
That Jesus rose from the grave—
Those soldiers had no clues!
The FLOWERS in my hands
Express joy on that glad day!
Jesus arose on Easter!—
And, He's washed my sins away!
The BIRDS were singing merrily
On that first glad Easter morning!
They burst in song so gaily—
Didn't give us any warning!

BUNNIES hopped around the place,
Sharing excitement with the rest—
Jesus loved the animals,
He probably loved these best!
The SUN does shine on Easter
To make us all feel good!—
No doubt, Jesus sends sunshine,
For I know He said He would!
BELLS are ringing merrily,
As they ring loud and clear,
That Jesus rose up from the tomb
"Glad Easter time is near!"
With FRIENDS all around us,
We'd like to share the story;
The Easter message we shall tell;
We can all meet Him in glory!

Note: The words in capital letters
designate the items they carry in
their hands—you know—show and tell!

Service for Palm Sunday

Matthew 21:7 They brought the donkey and the colt, placed their cloaks on them, and Jesus sat on them.

Jesus came into Jerusalem
On a donkey so small.
If Jesus seemed heavy,
It didn't mind at all!

A very large crowd spread their cloaks on the road, while others cut branches from the trees And spread them on the road. Matthew 21:8,9

Palm leaves were scattered;
They cast lots for them;
It was an honor for Jesus,
To have it done for Him!

Sing---"Palms" (Tune to "Jesus Loves Me"):
Let us wave our palms up high,
As the King comes passing by.
Little ones can wave them, too.—
Praising Him is what they do!
(Sing chorus of "Jesus Loves Me")

Then one of the twelve, Judas Iscariot, went to The chief priests and asked, "What are you willing to give me if I hand Him over to you? They counted out 30 pieces of silver for him! Matthew 26:14,15

Thirty pieces of silver was used
To betray our Jesus and Lord.
He was hated by the Romans,
But He's One whom we've adored!

"I tell you the truth", Jesus answered, "This very night
before the cock crows, you will deny me three times."
Matthew 26:34

Can't you hear the rooster crow,
As he takes part in it all?
It's a wake-up call, if we may,
May WE never resist God's call!

Very early in the morning, the chief priests,
the elders, and the teachers made a decision.
They bound Jesus and led Him away to Pilate.
Mark 15:1

Jesus was led in chains—
It seems so wrong, so dense,
For a man who was so innocent,
It just doesn't make sense!

They twisted a crown of thorns, and set it on
His head. When they crucified Him, they divided up His
clothes by casting lots.
Matthew 27:35

They placed on Jesus' head
Thorns from a bush—a crown,
A pair of dice suggests gambling,
For His clothes He'd laid down!

While they were eating, Jesus took bread,
gave thanks and broke it, and gave it to His
disciples, saying, "Take, eat, this is my body".
Then He took the cup, gave thanks, and
offered it to them, saying, "Drink from it,
all of you. This is my blood of the covenant,
which is poured out for many for the forgive-
ness of sins." Matthew 26:26, 27, & 28

Grapes are the symbol
Of the blood Jesus shed,
And the symbol for His body,
Is this slice of bread!

Then came the day of the unleavened bread on
which the Passover lamb had to be sacrificed.
Luke 22:7

The Feast of Unleavened Bread
Was a celebration in that day.
A lamb then was slain,
And prepared in a special way!

And being found in appearance as a man, He
humbled Himself, and became obedient to
death—even death on the cross.
Philippians 2:8

Jesus was crucified on a cross—
A most horrible death to die,
But He did it so willingly—
Never asked once, "Why?"

*So the other disciples told Him. "We have seen
the Lord!" But he said to them, "Unless I see the nail
marks in His hands, and put my fingers
where the nails were, and put my hands into His side,
I will not believe it!"*
John 20:25

Nails were driven in His hands
To hold His body in place.—
Can you imagine the agony,
That could be seen on His face?

*Joseph took the body and wrapped it in a clean
linen cloth. Matthew 27:59*

A clean piece of linen cloth
Was used to wrap Jesus carefully
As He was placed in the tomb;
Joseph of Arimathea did it prayerfully!

*Immediately one of them ran and got a
sponge. He filled it with wine vinegar,
put it on a stick,
and offered it to Jesus to drink.
Matthew 27:48*

He became thirsty while hanging
There waiting to die,
So a sponge dipped in cheap wine,
Was offered for His cry!

*When the Sabbath was over, Mary Magdalene,
Mary, the mother of Jesus, and Salome
brought spices so they might anoint His body.
Mark 16:1*

Whole cloves and other spices
Were used for anointing the dead,
But this was all unnecessary,
For He's risen as He said!

*"Don't be alarmed," he said, "You are looking
for Jesus of Nazareth, who was crucified. He
has risen! He is not here. See the place where
they laid Him! Mark 16:6*

I have an empty egg—
It represents the empty tomb!
If you haven't accepted Jesus,
In your heart, you'll have room!

(Adult choir sings: O come to my heart, Lord
Jesus. There is room in my heart for Thee.)

He's ALIVE!

"Easter Time is Here Again"
(tune to "Here Comes Peter Cottontail")

1st Verse:
Easter time is here again—
Pretty flowers, where've you been?—
Poppin' out on every sunny day!
Showin' every girl and boy,
Reasons we can sing for joy—
Songs to tell the living Savior's way!
He's got words that He's fulfilling,
He's got promises kept, too!—
And assurance for each grown-up
That we can accept as true!

Chorus:
Oh! Here is why we can't be sad—
Jesus rose to make us glad—
Glad we're saved this Happy Easter day!

2nd verse:
Jesus Christ arose that day—
Angels rolled the stone away!
Let's all stop and listen to Him say!—
"Try to do the things you should!"—
Maybe if you're extra good—
He will tell the world that you're O. K.
You'll wake up tomorrow morning—
And you'll know your life of sin,
Was forgiven and forgotten—
Until Jesus comes again!

Chorus:
Oh! Here is why we can't be sad—
Jesus rose to make us glad—
Glad we're saved this Happy Easter day!

Easter Means New Life!

Remember as you celebrate
At Easter time this year,
That flowers, candy, & colored eggs
Are lots of fun—that's clear!

But so much more important
Is the reason why we sing.—
Jesus died and rose again.—
It made the heavens ring!

Death no longer has control
Of those who have no doubt
That Jesus showed His perfect love,
That's what Easter's all about!

Have you decided to receive
Christ's Easter gift of love?
Confess your sin, believe, receive
This gift that's from above!

Easter means so many things,
I'm sure that you'll agree,
But what it means to our group here,
Is what I wanted to see.

I was surprised at the answers,
When I asked each to explain.
They were sincere in their thinking,
Yet they didn't rack their brain!

Some said they go away,
And worship with relatives and friends,
While others just stayed at home,
Or—it just all depends!

Some receive small gifts;
Usually something they needed to wear—
Like new white shoes for spring,
Or maybe a ribbon for their hair.

One said new cut grass comes
with Easter on some occasions;
Another remembered of snowy grass,
and chilly wind with no limitations!

The Easter bunny always came
to all with whom I conferred,
And he had eggs hidden around,
and the thought hadn't seemed absurd!

"I always had to learn a poem,
To say at one service or another"—
This came from two or three of my friends;
One was made to sing by her Mother!

One recalled of a service,
Where the twins got in a fight!
We laughed and had fun about this;
We agreed that this was all right.

All of these things were discussed,
But there is much more to be said;
Everyone gave in his very first breath,
"Why, Christ arose! And He is not dead"!

Christ arose and is living—
Each one explained to me;
This was foremost in their minds,
Which is the way it should be!

The fact that Christ died for them,
And has saved them from their sins,
Each realized this was salvation—
Each knew where salvation begins.

Praise the Lord for youth,
Who will make this important stand!
Praise the Lord for their witness—
May it spread throughout our land!

May we who are older take notice;
Be more Christlike because of their views!
If there were all BYF's put together,
These are the one's I'd choose!

New Life in April

In April, we find a newness of life;
We forget winter's cold; we forget worries and strife.
The flowers break the cold sod, and in colors, beauty sings,
Their silent praise to Christ, the risen King of Kings.
No worldly problems at this time, can dim the Christian's way,
For God's triumphant glory floods our lives each Easter day!
It means so much to us, Father, to have a risen Lord like you!
You've always been so helpful; you come when we ask you to!
So if I could give out any gift, I'd give much love and laughter,
A peaceful heart, a special dream, and joy forever after!

Baptism—Christopher

We want to celebrate with you on your baptism today.
We hold you up in prayer in a very special way!
We are proud to be a part of these wonderful celebrations!
May your precious life be filled with all your parents' loving expectations!

Love and best wishes from
Great Uncle Max and Great Aunt Nina

**"Faithful Stewards" (to the tune of
"Jesus Loves Me")**

Faithful stewards we shall be,
Light the way for all to see!
Take control of what we own,
Follow up on seed we've sown!

Yes, God will love us!
Yes, God will love us!
Yes, God will love us;
He's promised in His Word!

As the church participates—
Hope to enter Heaven's gates!
We'll love God with all our soul—
Love our neighbor is our goal!

God has blest me with a desire,
To play the piano and sing;
He also gave me the ability
To write poetry about everything!

So I praise Him for blessing me;
Helping me with all I do.
I just want to give God glory,
As I play this song for you!

Please turn to page 279;
I'll play it one time through;
Let's sing the last two verses,
I pray you'll enjoy that, too!

Section 6.
Time for Just Friends and Family

Many poems in this section have been created
with a need for a message on a birthday card,
inserts with gifts and anniversaries
or just fun times with friends and family.

Together it is time to exalt His name forever.
Psalm 34:4

Time for Friends

Gisele, you are a year older,
Let's celebrate in style—
What I'd like from you,
Is a great big smile!

Did you have a nice summer?
Ours really went fast—
We've been very busy—
Our energy doesn't last!

We've had ripe tomatoes,
They taste so good—
We're waiting for the corn—
We'd hurry that if we could!

Have you done any traveling?
Did you stay home all summer?—
We went to the State fair,
Which was quite a "bummer" (too hot)

We watched the cattle show—
An elephant ear was a treat!
I always enjoy caramel corn!—
There's always too much to eat!

Have you had tongue lately?—
Should we kill a cow?
We enjoy the steaks—
I can taste them now!

Enjoy your birthday!
Do what you like!
Go to a movie—
Take a ride on your bike!
(Come see us!) Love, Nina

To Tabitha—ABWM Scholarship student:

Here's some window cleaner
To help keep the place clean!
May you enjoy this product—
It's the best you've ever seen!

If you need more of this product,
Let me know on-line.
My e-mail is given below—
Just let me know, that's fine!

Happy Anniversary to our friends in Ireland:

May joy and peace be yours,
As you live your lives together,
May you have good health and happiness!
May you enjoy lots of sunny weather!

May 20, 2003—Traveling in Ireland:

Robert, you were a wonderful tour guide,
You explained everything so well.—
You made sure we enjoyed it—
I'm sure YOU did, as well!

This is a token of appreciation
And love from all of us!
We wish you what's best in life.
And safety in driving that bus!
From the Indiana passengers

TOUR GUIDE,
ROBERT LAMBERT

To Dick Phillips

Thanks for doing the "special",
When you had little time to plan!
Some are hard to depend on,
But, with you, I know I can!

May God bless you in all your endeavors,
Whether it's church, music, or work, too.
May you enjoy the life you deserve,
And do what you choose to do!

Happy Anniversary

We appreciate you two—
You've been the answer to our need!
Maybe you can't see all you've done,
But you've surely planted the seed!

To Mary Temple:

We love this time of year
When we can be together,
To share the fun and memories,
Regardless of the weather!

Here's a token of my love,
May it be a blessing to you—
And remind you of loving friends
Who appreciate what you do!

The food we had was delicious,
But the fellowship was even more fun!
The cookie cutter will be a joy to use,
And by Christmas, we shall all weigh a ton!
You're so loving! Happy Holidays!

Priorities

Let's talk about priorities,
Are my activities in line?
Is my day's schedule planned right?—
Is that a serious fault of mine?

I need to pray and meditate—
Should be first on my list,
But let me share all the duties,
As they come hand over fist!

As I tumble out of bed,
When the alarm has made its sound,
Plans are coming out of my head
Before I touch the ground!

I run, plug in the coffee pot,
After the bathroom musts are through.
I make the bed real quick like,
To get to the other things to do!

Oh, yes, throw in a little wash,
I'll need for work today,
Run the sweeper to pick up the lint
And whatever gets in the way.

And now to make a phone call,
Before Leah gets off to work.
Maybe I can talk to **Erika**,
A pleasure I cannot shirk.

And now, Lord, for the devotions,
But is my mind really for you?
You see, I've cluttered it with business—
With things I felt I should do!

I hurry to read <u>Our Daily Bread</u>,
Hunt the scripture that goes right along.
Oh, I hear the door bell ringing,
Has something gone wrong?

A neighbor came to remind me,
I had promised to help her today.
The best thing to do,
Is go right away!!

(Next day)
I shall start this day right.—
My Bible was near my bed.
I read <u>Our Daily Bread</u> and
Noticed what the scripture said.

It so happened the message was
To always put Jesus first;
Then the day was so different,
I was so happy I could burst!

The coffee even tasted better,
For it was perked just right,
In making my bed, I realized—
I didn't really have to fight.

The wash even became brighter,
At least, it seemed that way;
The phone calls from other people
Just seemed to make my day!

A little talk with **Erika**
Is as pleasant as can be;
All I need to hear
Is a little noise to me!

Now, since I started my day
With a talk with my Savior and Lord,
To start a day any other way—
I just really can't afford!

A Day With Rachel

Our 24 hours together
Is what this note is for.
The time kept passing fast;
I wish we could have had more!
These thoughts I'm wanting to share now
Are jumping around in my mind,
They're not in order of importance;
I'm just letting my heart unwind!
That little rake for gardening
Is so long past due;
For breaking crusty soil,
Helping vegetables to come through.
The barn boots we bought
Are just what I need,
I can sweep the parlor—
Or the calves, I can feed.
I felt so well-blest
And enjoyed seeing **Lou Ann**,
'Twas not a coincidence—
It was just God's plan!
Naomi was so sweet
To stop by for a minute,
If there's a crown for thoughtfulness,
I'm sure she'll win it!
The typewriter is super;
I love to use it
I used to have speed,
And I did lose it!
The toy for **Jeremy**
I just had to bring,
What kind of Grandma
Would not bring a thing?
I talked with **June** some,
but intended to be with her;
I was a little disappointed—
Rain put us in a dither!

Yes, we went jogging,
I really enjoyed that!
We talked of eliminating
Some of our fat!
Your loveliness and warmth
Is hard to forget—
I love you, you gave me
A shampoo and set!
While we went shopping,
We went to Hardee's to eat,
To enjoy others' cooking
Is sometimes hard to beat!
Delores and **Regi,**
You took me to see;
They had arms out,
How delighted it made me!
This was all because of
Jeff's quarter of beef,
Handling that kind of money—
I've turned over a new leaf!
Kenny just always
Makes me comfortable, too;
He checks my vehicle—
Something I can't seem to do!
This day we spent together
Surely was special to me!
I'll do it more often,
Just you wait and see!
Thanks for all of it;
I'll cherish it a lot.
It makes me realize
What a great sis I've got!

Special Times with Family
(Samples of thank you's and well-wishes)

Erika, if love for one being,
Kept that one healthy and strong,
We'd never need a doctor,
Our lives would be long!

For the price of your giving,
Can never be measured,
We sense how you love us—
This will always be treasured!

May your Christmas, **Erika**,
Be an exotic gem,
May your being in our family,
Make us want to serve Him!
Love from Gr & Gr

To All Mothers:

I'll bet she never thought before,
She would influence me forever!—
I'm proud of all she taught me—
She made an impressive endeavor!

So here's to all the mothers,
Whether living, or gone on ahead!—
Just stick to your mother's great wisdom,
And try to live as she said!

Donna, thinking of you!—
May your day be full of laughter,
Let joyful thoughts run thru your head!
Enjoy planning loving friendships,
Before you get ready for bed!

For, I'm saying a little prayer
For God's help to sustain you,
And give you all the strength you need
For what you're going through!

BJ—I don't send cards often,
But when I sit down to do it,
I try to make it pay,
So there's really nothing to it!

May your day be special,
As much as birthdays can be—
Years are counting up pretty fast,
At least, they are on me!

So, let's make the best of it,
Get out and make a few tracks,
Make someone else chuckle,
Put on a few fun-time acts!

Greg, I am very pleased and proud,
Of the blessing you've been to me!—
I think it's the most joy,
To have a grandson like Jeremy!
Love U, Mom

Cecil, you've been a good father,
And we appreciate all you've done!
Those children are most precious,
To us, they're such great fun!
We love U, Max & Mom

Nancy—May you in money-management,
Be successful in reaching high scores!—
And as you're helping so many—
May a lot of this some day be yours!
Love from Max & Mom

Jeremy—Another birthday is here—
It's time to celebrate!
You've been a good boy—
You've got a clean slate!

So take the day off—
Get a ticket to fly—
You won't have any fun,
If you really don't try!

Pick up your wife, **Julie**,
Go on a cruise,
Or something else exciting—
Whatever you choose!
Love from Grandma & Max

Tyler, you're on our minds a lot—
We're proud you're one of us,
So don't get so upset,
When we make a little fuss!

We are praying for good reports,
It's the least we can do!
We've asked the Lord to bless,
And take good care of you!
Love from Grandma and Max

More Time with Family & Friends

Rachel and Kenny, a message for you,
We're as grateful as can be
To travel west as we did,
And enjoy your company!

The sights we saw were heavenly—
'Twas God's beauty to behold,
But associating with those you love,
Makes it worth its weight in gold!

We'll remember this vacation,
For many years ahead.
We were treated so royally—
Not enough could be said!

I cut down on my sweetener,
To keep happiness about!
I'll always think of you, **Kenny**,
When I get the blue package out!

May we, if the Lord sees fit,
Go again somewhere soon!
We'll look forward to it!—
Should it be to the moon!

Love, from Max & Nina

Jeremy, come climb onto this birthday boat,
And blow your birthday horn,
Let's celebrate on November 9,
It's the day that you were born!
Exodus 33:14
Love from Grandma and Max

Ginny, I went shopping, to find a card that said:
Happy Birthday to a special sister-in-law;
None there, so I made this one instead!

You are very special; you mean a lot to me!
I wish you peace and happiness,
That will fill the deepest sea!

Dewey, my theme here is wild animals;
I know you love them, too!
So it's happy birthday in abundance,
From all of us to you!

Bill, you didn't have a birthday this year,
But I'm sending you this anyway!
Just enjoy this the whole week,
And act like every day is your day!
(February 29th)

Traveling

As we travel in the motor home,
From the West to the East.
The beauty of God's creation
Is phenomenal, to say the least!

There's so much we take for granted
On how well it's supervised.
There's evidence of wild life,
As though they've been hypnotized.

The highways are so well-marked,
It's easy—just follow the signs.
It really keeps us busy, though,
To read between the lines!

Dave Parks,

Your hospitality amazed us,
You showed us love every minute!
We could tell on our arrival,
You had put your heart in it!

May God bless your role in life,
And I don't know if you even knew it—
You can fill the void in **Rachel**'s life,
Better than anyone else can do it!

(**Dave**, you're an angel unaware—
We love you, Uncle Max & Aunt Nina)

To Nancy & Andy Juhasz

It was a joy to be in your home!—
It's hard to believe it was true,
That we could come together again,
Yes, from childhood, I idolized you!

Thank you for your hospitality,
Hope it wasn't a strain for you two!
May God bless you with good health,
As only He can do! Love Max & Nina

Twila and Dave,

You were married on the 5th of August—
That was the day I married your Uncle Ray;
That is how I can remember your anniversary—
Hope you two have a wonderful day!
In Jesus' love, Max & Nina

Time Out, **Tyler**—
Hope you have a lot of fun
On your birthday this year!
Yes, we're rooting for you
With a great big cheer!
GOOOOO, **Tyler**, Slam—Dunk!

Coffing Sisters' Weekend

Each year in the autumn
When summer's winding down,
We five sisters, the Coffings
Take a trip out-of-town!

This year was no exception—
We all got together;
And toured Central Indiana—
We did have good weather!

The four of us in the north—
On a Friday, as we traveled south,
Ate at Al's—it was the best
That you could put in your mouth!

Now, on Eagle's Watch Drive,
The home of sister **Joan**,
We had our Christmas exchange—
It's the only time we can!

Pacer sweatshirts were given,
By no other than Joan.
These gifts—quite appropriate,
For she's quite the Pacer fan!

Ornaments from sister, **Betty**,
Of the Old Stone House near Peru,
Where our Mother lived when small,
We will cherish these, too!

Rachel gave tatted hankies,
Made by a lady age 104,
Who died the very next day—
This was her last chore!

June gave us banners,
We can keep our colors flying—
Our character will be revealed—
Without our half trying!

Recipe books were given,
Books on golf, quilting, and all—
To go along with our hobbies—
We really had a ball!

Our history lesson this weekend
Was Battleship Indianapolis and its plight!—
Then to nursing home in Greenwood,
With Esther Coffing we had a bite!

Really, it was a lovely lunch,
Ate privately and enjoyed our stay,
Talked genealogy and toured the Home—
Could have stayed all day!

We went to Circle City Mall—
Shopped 'til we ran out of money,
Enjoyed the beauty of up-town life—
Got lost and it wasn't funny!

Chinese food in the evening—
We were served at Ching Ming Fu.
Had no idea what we ate,
But I'm sure the Chinese do!

Joan served us both breakfasts—
Didn't jog because of the weather;
Then to worship at Grace Brethren Church,
To top off the weekend together!

We took **Cousin Ella** a cake
For her birthday this year,
But we missed a visit with her,
We didn't even get to see her!

The Colts were playing that day—
Joan has season tickets for those,
So we came back home to relax—
Had fun, more than anyone knows!

We look forward to this event,
It keeps us all intact!—
God has blest us in this endeavor—
We all know this for a fact!

Fall of 1993

Coffing Sisters 1996

The Coffing sisters got together again
Like we do every year,
To catch up on yearly happenings;
These events we hold dear!

The weekend started on Friday;
From the north came **Rachel** and **June**,
Picking up **Nina** in Rochester,
Hoping **Betty** would be ready soon!

Her customers want to be beautiful,
So she tried to please them all.
We hurried them out the door,
For fear of another call!

We four ate supper together
At AL's of Logansport, out 29.
We always enjoy eating there;--
One of the better places to dine!

We four put our funds together
To get a hospitality gift for **Joan**.
How can you go wrong with flowers?
We agree it's the best plan.

As we gathered with **Joan** in Indy,
Our evening was spent with sharing,
For this is a time for Christmas exchange
And discuss what each is wearing!

Much of the evening was spent giggling.
Heard of honeymoon of Nina and Max.
She shared all about Ireland,--
Tried to share the most interesting facts!

Saturday was spent in Greenwood,
With a Coffing relative who's 93!
We had a great discussion on genealogy.—
Esther's as sharp as she can be!

We stopped in super outlet stores—
What gal doesn't enjoy shopping?
Then to Beef & Boards for the evening;-
'Twas the weekend's "cake's best topping."

We sat with a gentleman at dinner,
More entertainment than we bargained for.
The gentlemen there furnished excitement!
Couldn't have asked for more!

We had a good night's rest with **Joan**,
We went to a church that morning.
Left **Joan** for she had Colts tickets;
She had already given us that warning!

We are thankful for these weekends,
We look forward to them a lot!
We praise God for this blessing,
And for the precious sisters we've got!

Sister's Weekend 1997

It's that time of year, friends,
For the Coffing sisters to get out and go.
We look forward every year,
And enjoy it more than you know.

We started early on Friday evening,
Leaving from **Betty**'s beauty shop.
I drove my van this time;
It's easy to start and stop.

Our first stop was at Al's diner—
Fine dining at its best;
This stop is getting traditional,
There's a special treatment for each guest.

We have fun buying flowers
For **Joan** who serves as our hostess,
Always lays out the welcome mat—
Charm and elegance, she has the "mostess"!

We enjoy our Christmas exchange;
We do it early each year;
For, you see we're busy at Christmas,
Enjoying the others we hold dear!

Colts sweatshirts were given,
Personalized stationery, neat vases,
Tree ornaments were appreciated,
As were embroidered pillow cases.

A family tree was a gift,
Honoring the genealogist craze.
Home canned peaches were shared—
That's work of many days!

Thimbles, lighthouses, birdhouses,
Honoring those who have collections.—
What an exciting gift exchange,
All of which were thoughtful selections.

But more importantly we shared,
What only sisters do discuss!
Silly secrets and jokes are told—
These don't go beyond us!

We went to Danville, Indiana,
On Saturday to the applefest.
There were fruit and food items in places,
There were craft items in all the rest.

To Covington, Indiana, we traveled
To the apple festival there!—
It was a fun trip, too,
Bought as much as we'd dare!

We visited the Coffing Brothers' Fruit Market,
Now that was a pleasant surprise.
Our genealogist sisters traced back—
Found we were related to those guys!

We didn't go to a theater that night.—
We were ready to call it a day;
Had a good meal and hit the sack—
As we grow older, we act that way!

Sunday morning was fun, as usual—
We found a church to give God praise
For giving us so many blessings;
We always feel like it pays!—

For each of us felt His presence,
From the worship, and one was baptized!
The call from the minister in charge—
Found this new life—we weren't surprised!

The children's moments were quite different;
The leader carved a pumpkin for this reason;
Didn't make a devil's face, but a cross—
Explaining Jesus being Light of the harvest season!

We had a 10:30 brunch at Boat Yard;
This closed sisters' weekend gate.—
We're thankful we still get together;
We're ready to do it again in '98!

Sister's Weekend—1999

On the first day of October,
'Twas Friday about 1:00,
The Famous Five Coffing Sisters
Left for a weekend of fun!

Rachel and **June** from Mishawaka
Stopped in Rochester for **Nina**,
Then for **Betty**, near Twelve Mile,
Were we running late?—Kinda!—

For, you see, as we get older
We try to plan right—
Do most driving during the day,
And not so much at night!

We had supper in Logansport,
We tried to save up for later,
Purchased flowers and a fruit basket
To treat those who cater—

They cater to us girls—
Yes, nearly everyone we meet,
For when they see us together,
They all think it's neat!

Food at Happy Burger West
Was, as always, the best—
On to **Joan**'s in Indy
To consider getting rest.

Well, it came to be late—
And not a good story was missin'—
All seemed to be talking—
There was no one to listen!

We each are a sounding board
To get things off our chest,
When that is caught up,
Then we can rest!

This is Christmas for us,
To exchange gifts!—Remember?
We do this in October, since
We're with our families in December!

Joan came up with an idea—
She gave us work to do!
Tulip bulbs, daffodils, hyacinths,
Crocuses, a planter, and guide, too!

Even fertilizer spikes!—
Let's not take her for granted!—
We'll see **Joan** all over the yard,
If we get them all planted!

Betty worked hard all summer,
Canning from her garden that grew,
Shared jam, apple butter and pear butter,
Salsa, crab apples, and canned chicken, too!

Rachel's gifts were practical, too,
A watch, handmade by her friend,
A letter opener she got in Alaska—
On her we can always depend!

June had Y2K in mind—
She gave as our parents taught her—
Jelly beans, a flashlight, and peaches,
A can opener, toilet paper, and water!

Lumber had been stored at the Warner's,
From trees that had fallen in the past.—
This was cut into small wooden pieces
And made into hanging baskets that will last!

This was a delightful time to share,
But we got to bed really late.
Then **Joan** came up with that big breakfast,
We surely didn't lose any weight!

Saturday we traveled to Metamora!
This was a neat experience, no less!
This little town was full of little shops—
We did much shopping, we'll confess!—

And I did!—I set my purse down
To pose for a picture to be taken.—
I found an EMT standing over my purse,
Calling Security!—Man, was I shakin'!

We headed over to Boggstown
For the dinner and evening show.
It was filled to capacity, but we had a ball!—
You can't appreciate all that, 'til you go!

I wanted to play the piano,
But it didn't work out that way—
Their pianists were so phenomenal,
So it's just as well,
I'll try some other day!

We all went to church in Greenwood.
Joan's friend, **Peg**, welcomed us there.
The minister spoke with authority and wisdom,
The people all showed passion and care!

We arrived at Greenwood Village Lane—
Met **Esther**, at 95, going strong.
We had a good lunch, fun visiting—
She says we stay away too long!

We exchanged e-mail numbers
and took pictures
Of Coffings standing in line!
We give praise to God for the memories!—
Enjoyed sister's weekend—'99!

February 25, 2004

Sisters' Weekend, 2000

The "famous five" did it again—
We staged our weekend fling.
Joan planned it all as usual,
But we really did our own thing!

The seventh of October of year 2000
Was the date of this event.
We ate supper in Logansport
At "Bob Evans" before we went.

All night at **Joan**'s was exciting!
We exchanged gifts like we always do.
See, we're busy with families at Christmas,
So this makes it more memorable, too!

June gave us all tree ornaments,
And goodies too numerous to mention.
Genealogical comments from her
Were what really kept our attention!

Rachel was busy on her computer,
Created a calendar, beautifully done!
For each month through the year,
She used recent pictures or an old one!

Betty canned food all summer,
Gave chicken, all kinds of jelly, or about,
And a microwave pan, so practical,
Makes us not to want to eat out!

Joan's gift to each of us
Was a ticket to "Mystery Café"
Had a 5-course meal, took part in their act,
Computer terms were the order of the day!

I enjoy my computer, too—
Made greeting cards for all through the year.
I tried to think of things THEY enjoy,
As they send them to those they hold dear!

We visited **Esther Coffing** on Saturday—
She laid out the welcome mat at noon,
Had a good meal at Greenwood Village—
Visiting TIME went all too soon!

Thelma, Carlene, and **John**
Helped celebrate the reunion that day—
We kept in touch with relatives!
It's lots of fun to do it this way!

We toured Conseco Field House with **Tyler,**
(He's my grandson who works there.)
He seemed proud to guide us through—
He escorted us everywhere!

The Congressional Medal of Honor Memorial
Was a fantastic sight to see.
It displays, uniquely, names of those
Who gave their lives in war, so heroically!

The Christ Church Cathedral on the Circle
Was where we attended Sunday at 10:00.
We ate lunch and then were homebound.
We'll probably do it next year again!

It's a tradition we enjoy each year.
We look forward to it a lot!
God has blest us to be able to do this,
We praise Him for the good health we've got!

This poem was composed by Nina—
I'm the middle of this Coffing "bunch"!
This is the 12th year we've done this,
Mom and Dad would be proud, I've a hunch!

February 25, 2004

Sisters' Weekend 2001

'Twas the twelfth of October
In two-thousand one,
Not a sister of the Coffings,
Was not ready to have fun!

June and **Rachel** left home at three,
For me at Rochester at four-thirty,
Betty was ready when she made
All her customers "perty".

We stopped at "Hap's" in Logansport
To get a bite to eat.
We had rain to Indianapolis
Before **Joan** we would meet.

My! What a scramble we all had
To get gifts ready for each one!
You see, we exchange gifts each year—
Most looked-forward-to tradition, bar none!

However, today is **Joan**'s birthday,
So we took her a cake.
Well, nobody wanted to eat it,
So that was a mistake!

June's been busy as can be
Getting genealogy for us to be aware,
That each of our notebooks include
Our ancestry history laid out with care.

Since, to be patriotic
Is what we all want to be,
June gave us flag pins
To wear prominently.

Rachel created a similar program;
Sisters' weekends she printed clear
In a loose leaf notebook,
Including other events of each year.

Rachel then took a sisters picture,
Had it on a T-shirt displayed.
It makes us proud to be family—
A part of the Coffing parade!

Betty spent time in her kitchen,
Prepared garden produce she had canned,
My "green" bag contained it all;
We claimed the color she had planned.

She also gave us a devotional book
To each of us to read,
A cup labeled "Farmerette Beauty Barn",
To use and travel with at any speed.

Joan's gift to us contained essentials
We found lovely and useful, as well,
In a lovely basket, even reusable—
It will enhance my home, I can tell.

I had planned to fly to Ireland
On the fifteenth of September
To select Belleek china,
To give a gift they'd remember.

A phone call from Aerlingus Airlines
Came to us after the "attack",
Reporting that no flights would be leaving,
For we might not get back.

SO, my gifts were from **Leah**,
Who holds "Country Peddler" shows.
She helped choose gifts for her Aunts,
And usually a loving niece knows.

For **Rachel**, a lighthouse tapestry piece,
For **Joan**, a rooster-door-stop to display,
For **Betty**, a candle-lit wind gauge,
For **June**, a neat paper-towel holder,
     of light gray.

Joan got up early Saturday morning—
Her hospitality showed grace as before,
She set out a lovely breakfast—
A casserole and fresh fruit galore!

We decided to go shopping—
We all needed to do that.
June and **Rachel** needed shoes and jewelry—
Betty needed a new hat!

We met **Peggy Collect**, **Joan**'s friend—
She seems like our sister, too.
She helps us to have a good weekend
No matter what activity we do!

We always see Cousin **Esther**,
She is close to ninety-eight.
John and **Carlene** put off going to Florida,
So that our plans with **Esther** were straight!

Thelma, a cousin, met with us,
Brought her dog, **"Buttons"**, too.
He seems like a good companion—
Bringing him along was the thing to do!

We try to cheer **Esther** with fruit,
And she appreciates it a lot,
But visiting and picture-sharing is better
Than anything else we've got!

It was a gloomy day to sight-see,
But we really made the best OF it.
We went to the Miniature
Doll-House in Carmel,
We all really did love it!

Then we called **Tyler**, my grandson,
To get tickets for the Pacer game.
He did that for no cost to us—
Now, wouldn't that be a shame—

If we gave him nothing in return?
He said, "Grandma, I like peach pie, myself".
"No problem", I said to him,
As I took a quart of peaches from the shelf.

The Pacers lost, but we had good seats,
The evening turned out to be fun!—
Got back to good night's rest
At **Joan**'s before the next day's sun.

Sunday morning, our church service
Was at the Baptist on Raceway Road.
The church was small, but the message
was mighty—
The minister said, "Look to the SCARS
& STRIPES as our mode".

We ate at CHILI's for lunch—
Going home time is now near.
We praise God for our great times, always,
Planning already for next year.

Graduates Of 50 Years, May Of '93

Dear graduate, many years have passed,
Since your graduation day!
Many things have happened,
'Cause the world is made that way!
While going to school at Metea,
You learned the Golden Rule,
But there are those who object now,
To have this taught in school!
You were given homework,
Like kids talk about today,
But the work wasn't studying,
It was mow yard and make hay!
You carried your lunch to school,
Consisting of gardening one grows,
But now our kids have perfect lunches,
And sometimes they turn up their nose!
I'll bet you never heard of drug abuse,
The drugs you took were for a cold—
Whiskey, a little coal oil, and some sugar—
You drank this when you were told!
Did you protest or have demonstrations?
I can just imagine a few of them—
You demonstrated how to plow corn,
Or showed a sister how to put in a hem!
Women's lib wasn't heard of in the twenties;
You hesitated to state your mind,
You probably said a few things under your breath,
Since you were the average kind!
Oh! There were no bathroom problems,
Not the scouring and cleaning, and who knows!
Invited guests never peered in the room,
Unless an unplanned situation arose!

The books and magazines in your day,
Held knowledge most dignified and true.
But there's a change in reading available,
If you check the latest "Ingenue".
The love-making had in your day,
Were by letters or notes to your beaus!
Today, kids kiss and hug in the halls,
And couldn't care less who knows!
In your day, there were teachers,
Who were dedicated to the task!
Some now teach for a reason that,
I'm almost afraid to ask!
While we are down to the nitty-gritty,
Here's one thing I should mention;
We get wrapped up in our own thing,
And let what's important get no attention!
There are complaints of all the high prices,
But wasn't it hard for your clan—
To give 50 or even 75 cents,
For your books, when the year began?
A lot could be said of the changes,
Between your school days and now.
We cannot forget that it's progress,
And sometimes we wonder how!
But, to you who are honored tonight,
May the best that God has to give,
Be yours to enjoy to its fullest,
And remain as long as you live!

Section 7.
Cruises

This is more fun times with family and friends.

The seas have lifted up, O Lord, the seas have lifted up their voice; the seas have lifted up their pounding waves. Psalm 93:3

It is a good time to praise the Lord. Psalm 92:1

Riviera—Cruise—3 sisters—Jan 05

Three sisters and their mates
Made plans to take a cruise,
Where the weather is warmer—
Was the best one to choose.

In January of 2005,
Seemed the most compatible date,
Avoiding doctor's appointments and all—
This time would be just great!

Our brother-in-law, **Ed Lewis**
Had a five by-pass surgery unexpected,
And we felt first things should be first,
So, visiting him was not neglected!

We gathered in Indy at **Joan**'s home,
To fly to Chicago, then LA—
Connections were made quite efficiently—
Boarded Norwegian Star, same day!

At Indy, snow and ice and bad plumbing
Caused us to have to switch planes!—
That probably started the mix-up—
Hence, lost luggage caused us pains!

We shared, made do, did washing,
Purchased necessary items on the ship!—
This was a true test of patience!—
Ask **Joan**, she nearly let one slip!

We kept saying, "Oh, what's the difference?"
We're on vacation and we'll probably get by!
God has a plan—it could be worse—
There is no need for us to ask "why?"

The Pacific Ocean was calm—
We had smooth sailing going south!
Sunrises and sunsets on water
Caused PTL to come from our mouth!

It's totally unbelievable,
Unless you experience one of these.
The indescribable beauty of God's handiwork,
Causes us to get on our knees!

Our rooms on the ship were elaborate,
We had room service, what a crew!
The ship had over 2,000 passengers—
Plus, the 1200 crew members, too!

It was a learning experience for us;
The culture was displayed, you could tell!
A few seemed rich—many were poor!—
Tour guides explained it well!

We took our digital camera
To film all sights we viewed!—
Went whale-watching, shopped on shore,
And there was never a lack of food!

The sunrises and sunsets were spectacular!—
The mountains, sea, sky, and flowers!
All of God's creation was available!—
One could just film and film for hours!

It was good to get to call home
For an update on everyone there!—
Dialed 092 and then a needed number;
From our room, I could call anywhere!

The gals at the cruise desk were magnificent!—
Accommodating whatever my need.
This made my "stay" on the ship,
A most enjoyable vacation indeed!

We recommend this delightful lifestyle
To anyone who is able to go!
Just absorb all of God's beauty
Before your age and your cash says, "No"!

P.S. I forgot to explain the lost luggage!—
On Wednesday, it caught up with us!
Since the hassle WAS repairable,
We really shouldn't make such a fuss!

January, 2005

A Vacation in Branson, Missouri

In September of 2000
We got our luggage together—
We count it continued honeymoon,
And it was just beautiful weather.

Shirley and Bill got our tickets
For some of the Branson shows—
Should have taken more notes,
But you know how that goes!

The showing of "The Promise"
The announcement of Jesus' birth—
Then, a story of the life of Jesus—
His life and death here on earth.

Shirley's nephew had a role—
Played the part of a Pharisee,
Who doubted Jesus' kingship,
Over all humanity.

We were proud of **Larry**,
He played his part well!
He hopes to obtain a better part,
He'd be excellent with "Jesus", I can tell!

Wednesday, we saw "Country Tonite"—
A display of talent, at its best,
The comedian—I laughed 'til I hurt,
Made me forget all the rest!

Thursday morning, we saw "Jennifer",
Featuring talent of dancing and singing.
She made it easy to love her,
By all the joy she was bringing!

Yakov Smirnof was phenomenal—
American citizen, but Russian by birth;
He slipped out of Russia—
Became an American of great worth!

His money didn't make him happy,
Making others happy?—Yes!
Americans were loving and giving—
He wanted to be that way, no less!

He had us all in tears,
Before we went out the door;
We're more proud to be an American,
Than we ever were before!

As he gave his presentation,
Many times he would say
That we had a peculiar understanding,
For we "never thought of it that way"!

We had shopped at the Bass Pro Shop
In Springfield, Missouri going down.
What a beautiful display of wildlife
And growth in air, sea, and on ground!

For those who hunt, fish, and trap,
'Twould be enjoyment for days.
For all those items you need or want,
Traveling all that far, pays!

We found time for extra walking,
To keep our bodies healthy.
Larry and **Karen** helped curb our expenses,
And we came home nearly as wealthy!

The Lord blest us all day long
With good weather, good fun, and good food!
When you ask for all this and get it,
It leaves us with a good attitude!

If you've a chance to go to Branson,
Do go and see what's there!
A fun-filled week here, at our age,
I have an idea, it's quite rare!

Heifer Project International

Heifer Project International,
I had never known about.
To realize world hunger?
Yes, I would take this route.

A chartered bus from Goshen
Picked us up at eight.
We headed towards Little Rock,
Each stop was never late.

Our bus driver, **Woody**,
With whom we could relax,
Made it enjoyable constantly,
And at times, gave out some facts!

A state trooper stopped us,
And asked us why the hurry;
Knowing **Woody**, he'd reply,
"Sir, you need not worry."

Pam performed her duties,
Brought little **Erin** along.
Efficient secretarial deeds
Were why not much went wrong!

Bill Alvey, our director,
Made us aware of HPI;
To relieve world hunger,
Answered each what and why!

Prayer partners were decided,
Wonderful way to get acquainted.
We mingled and tried to find out
How our life pictures were painted!

I found some—colorful,
I found lovely personalities.
It was exciting to realize—
These people were realities.

So we prayed for each other,
As the tour did progress,
We're nearly too busy learning,
We will have to confess.

Heifer Project International
Has Christlike groundwork laid.
We felt the Spirit's presence,
As each emphasis was made.

It was forty years ago—
West's efforts weren't in vain—
He set out to help the needy,
In this great sharing chain.

To start this great endeavor
From a cow in your dairy herd,
Her heifer calf is given,
For, "giving" is the word.

This calf will be a cow,
And produce milk for the owner,
But when it mothers a heifer calf,
She immediately becomes a donor.

This thrust is extended
To the hungry worldwide,
As hands reach out in want,
There's not one denied!

Now, some places, this heifer,
You'd not want to leave her,
You send other kinds of animals
To best benefit the receiver.

A cow wouldn't fit
In a crowded home in Japan,
But a chicken could lay eggs
Next to the frying pan.

There would not be grazing
For a cow, north, where it's cold,
But, bunnies cuddle and produce,
Until they get very old!

Even a mother goat would give
Some milk—keeping good taste
For a family of four
And none would go to waste.

Mother pigs produce litters—
Male and female, growing,
Meat of males are cured to eat,
While females keep business going!

In a mother duckling's home
There'd be ideally lots of water,
Hence—meat or eggs to eat,
Or an egg would make a daughter.

While we were traveling,
And to make the time go faster,
We played games for prizes,
Conducted by the pastor.

Uno, skipbo, and dice games
Were played now and then,
Kept sharp our concentration,
I count this no sin!

The Saturday night banquet
Was the highlight event!
After a delightful meal,
The evening was well spent.

Senator Bumper didn't make it,
For reasons as long as a mile,
But the others on the program
Made it all worth while!

Representatives from all regions,
States, provinces, and sections
Gave reasons we're proud
To have any connections.

We were encouraged to encourage
To give some of our supply
To the starving nations,
Before so many people die.

There were two evenings of relaxing
At Petit Jean State Park.
We tried to get settled
In our cabins before dark.

Calls were made to home,
Making sure we were missed;
And hearing a word from **Jeremy**,
I just couldn't resist!

We sang songs we knew,
That was part of our fun.
To make more noise than the rain
Is what we had done.

We revealed our prayer-partners
At supper Monday night.—
Nothing wrong was said,
For it was all so right!

Birthdays were celebrated,
We sang and had a cake.
Dorothy and **Willard** were surprised,
For a bow they had to take.

The six days are finished,
But our work's just begun,
To feed a hungry neighbor,
May we fail to reach none!

As we seek God's guidance,
As we promote this endeavor,
May we keep distributing
For heifer and forever!

Alaskan Celebrity Cruise—June, 1999

We shall share our experience
Of our exciting Alaskan vacation!
It was quite a thrilling adventure
To see God's majestic creation!

For there were sights we viewed,
I shall explain if I can—
The beauty and awesome magnitude
Of God's great and mighty plan!

We left early on Friday morning
For O'Hare airport by bus.
This vehicle was labeled
Especially for the 23 of us!

By air, we reached Seattle—
Had to adjust to the different time zone.
That was an important factor,
When we needed to use the phone!

Then, on to Seward, Alaska
To board the Celebrity Cruise ship,
With all of its luxuries and elegance—
What a way to take a trip!

Mercury was our ship's name—
2000 it would accommodate.
It was thirteen decks high—
Most luxurious in the state!

We dined in such a fashion,
That I wasn't accustomed to—
There was such a display of silverware—
And my habits require so few!

We were assigned to a table
To be used all the time aboard.
We had waiters and hosts—
These guys, we adored!

What we wanted or needed,
They went to get it, or do it!—
We were treated so royally—
A glance and they'd hop to it!

Our waiter was from the Philippines—
Got to know him quite well!—
Had a wife and two daughters—
Was a good father, you could tell!

His name is **Doods Maturingan,**
Felt he was the best!
He never slowed down any—
Just never stopped to rest!

We are in prayer for him,
As we remember his persistence.
A more conscientious man
Is not even in existence!

The cruise ship sailed the shore line—
Moved from port to port each night.
We toured these on buses
Or on a different way that was right.

We arrived in Juneau, the capitol,
Were impressed with what we saw.
You must see it to believe it—
I can't describe it all!

By train we left Skagway,
And enjoyed an exciting three hours.
A railway on cliffs, unbelievable,
Through tunnels, curves—exotic flowers.

We stopped at the scenic city of Sitka—
North America's largest city, they say,
At least, it covers more territory—
None other is laid out that way.

Each morning, walking was fun,
So after walking about a mile,
Max viewed from the Navigator's Club,
And I played the piano for a while!

We got to know our fellow travelers,
Whom we hadn't really known before.
These were a joy to be with—
We'd like to go cruising some more!

Rachel and **Kenny** had invited us—
They're who we dearly love.
Kenny's sister **Ann** and husband, **Gordon**
Made sure we were well taken care of!

Phyllis and Don White were our leaders,
They gave us such loving attention—
Made sure we had fun, whether they did or not—
(They'll have heavy crowns, I might mention!)

Joyce and **Forrest Frederick**
Are a couple we shared what we know!
She's a good extension homemaker—
And together to meetings, we shall go!

Ruth Perkins, and her son, **Scott**—
Always the two at our table,
Very interesting, to say the least—
Positive thinkers is their label!

Sarah Evans brought her grandson, **Ben**,
Now, isn't that idea neat?—
He treated her so royally,
And for her, he was a treat!

Merle and **Marie Thomas**
Were two we enjoyed with concern,
They were so carried away with events,
They nearly forgot to return!

Celia Detrick was a blessing—
She didn't complain any.
Phyllis and **Don** wheeled her around—
Hear of ones with such concern?—not many!

Art and **Theweah Hartig**
Were fun, down-to-earth folks—
Gave us a lot to laugh about—
At times shared a few jokes!

One piece of their luggage
Got lost on the home flight!
It came about two days later—
We thought perhaps it might!

Paul and **Alice Milslagle**
Made an atmosphere of fun!
You can tell they enjoy life
As much as anyone under the sun!

Sarah Lawall and **Carol Van Steen**
Were our mother-daughter combination.
Sarah appreciated her, and **Carol** was dedicated
To see her Mom enjoy a vacation!

Everyone had a camera—
We escaped photographers, if we could,
For they were always taking our picture,
Then you buy it, if it was good!

On our tour to Sitka
We saw Russian dancers in green.
These were volunteering young mothers
Sharing their dancing routine!

Also, there in Sitka, we visited
The Greek Orthodox Church so tall,
There were no pews for worship,
But I thought we just hadn't seen it all!

The cruise involved us constantly
In projects to make it such fun.
We associated with considerate citizens—
Complaints seldom heard by anyone!

Except for the last day or so—
And I find this quite amusing—
We filled out evaluation forms
To make improvements for future cruising!

Well, since there were 2000 aboard this ship,
Only a small % spoke English well,
Announcements and instructions were confusing,
When to do what, was hard to tell!

In Ketchikan, totem poles were carved—
This tour was enjoyed in the rain!
The tour guide was so helpful—
I can't believe all this in one brain!

Arts and craft classes were available,
Played bingo with prizes to keep—
Dancing and aerobics were offered,
We could even go to our room and sleep!

A helicopter ride was taken by some,
To the top of the glaciers to get a view.
We didn't take that ride that day—
We found other fun things to do!

This cruise was a marvelous treat;
We're grateful to God when we pray,
"Thanks, we've enjoyed Your handiwork,
May we enjoy it more each day!"

Cruise explained at an ABWM Meeting:

We shall share our cruise to Alaska—
Hit the highlights here and there!
We would, however, want to show,
How MISSIONS could be in the air!

For everywhere we go on this earth,
God's people are in every place.
We can promote Jesus' love for others
As we meet them face to face!

As we toured Alaska
Our chances there were many,
Of people who had firm religious belief,
Or even if they had any!

There were fellow travelers, tour guides,
And people promoting their wares—
Many showed signs of happiness—
Some had worrisome cares.

So, as we view the sights,
May we keep in the back of our mind—
We can lift in prayer those in need of it—
The unsaved are not hard to find.

Our tape lasts about 30 minutes—
Max tried to sort out the best.
Let's think of missions as we view this,
Let's not concentrate on the rest!

We were treated royally
As if we're King and Queen—
From the main attractions,
To all those in between!

To close, let us pray—
Father, we are so very thankful
For the beauty of this vast universe!
We feel a great responsibility
To count it a blessing—not a curse!

May the beauty of what we've seen,
Cause us to adore and worship more!
How responsible we are as your children—
To be in charge of what you have in store!

We are so convinced that you love us,
Within your majesty we want to cling!
We have no problem of claiming you—
To be our Savior, our Master, our King!

Fun Cruising on the Royal Caribbean Cruise Ship—Nordic Empress

Cruising on the Caribbean
Is an experience I'll never forget!
I felt God's presence in it all!—
Man hasn't created the likeness yet!

Air-travel is changing daily,
Security measures are gigantic!
We eagerly abide by these regulations!
Yes, terrorists must be getting frantic!

It is awesome to realize the number
Of the people who are traveling the earth!
The price we pay, though, is so minimal,
When you try to estimate its worth!

I sensed the vastness of the seas,
As we submarined 100 feet below,
To watch the sea-life creation,
And how little of what we know!

The Nordic Empress was our ship's name,
And sailing on this huge boat,
We spent much time on the water—
How could this weight stay afloat?

Many hundreds of crew workers
Made sure we sailed with ease!—
From cleaning, scrubbing, or cooking—
Never failed to say "Thank you" & "Please"!

Jerome was fantastic for our stateroom.
He was always, "Johnny on the spot"!
He did for us special favors,
When I'm sure others would not!

Maureen and Ron are friends we met
When we came to the table to eat.
It seems like we've known them forever—
Such friends are hard to beat!

We had a chance to lay in the sun,
And we could walk on deck #6.
Four times around was a mile—
We did it for health—not for kicks!

We were informed on a loud speaker,
As each scheduled program took place!
I was impressed with the organization—
Was pleased with each pleasant face!

On Sunday morning, we enjoyed church—
A denominational service for all!
It wasn't crowded at that time of day.
Our speaker hailed from Montreal!

One night was formal—
We tried to look our best!
Some looked spectacular,
And some just passed the test (my test)!

There was a deck to go shopping,
There was quite a choice to buy!
We could use a credit card or cash!
I thought the prices were a little high!

We had our favorite waiters!
Roarner and **Meriam** waited our table!
They treated us like royalty! To make
Us happy, they did what they were able!

Photographers were busy
To make memorable this occasion.
We heard accents from home and abroad,
And we tried to guess what nation!

An ice cream cone could always be had,
And to say "No", we've been trained!
We're on a guilt trip
For every pound we gained!

We docked at the capitol of Belize!
None such poverty have I seen!
Then to Cozumel off Mexico's coast—
Their mountains and hills were so green!

On Friday a passenger became ill—
A helicopter came to his aid,
Took him into Key West—where
Arrangements for his recovery were made!

I took advantage of a massage therapist,
To treat arthritis in my shoulder!
This was expensive, but worth it—
I can use that knowledge growing older!

Rachel, Kenny, Walt, and **Joan**,
Are family we enjoyed with the cruise!
With all this fun and excitement—
What is there to lose?!!

The weather on our cruise was beautiful—
The temperature stayed ideal!
The God who's in charge of it all,
Knows how to make His own feel!

Bitter cold and snow at home,
Wasn't the news we were glad about.
Cecil plowed our snow, turned up the heat,
This, we were NOT sad about!

I am so thankful we can travel,
And we have plans to do more—
To enjoy God's great universe,
Is what He created it for!

Cruise taken—
January 24th to the 31st, 2004
Max, Nina, Rachel, Kenny, Joan & Walt

Nordic Empress - Royal Caribbean Cruiseship

Cruising in International Elegance— CIE Tour of Ireland

May 5ᵗʰ to May 15ᵗʰ, 2002

Tour Guide and Bus Driver—Michael Hogan
A Creative Irish Gifts promotion
Conducted and managed by Kate & Greg Naples

If you ever go across the sea to Ireland,
You'll be convinced that God is on His throne,
For man could not create such beauty,
Even with all the technology he has known!

When you go, get **Michael** for a guide—
He will explain and drive carefully as he goes.
He gives history including dates, places and people—
To grasp it all, you must be on your toes!

On May 5ᵗʰ, 2002, it was a non-stop flight,
From O'Hare to Dublin, just seven and one-half hours.
Berkeley Hotel was waiting for our stay—
A well-planned tour gave us time to "smell the flowers"!

Kate and **Greg Naples** were in charge of it all—
Through a "Creative Irish Gifts" promotion.
And working with CIE Tours International—
Takes lots of dedicated planning and devotion!

We knew many details in advance,
So we could let our friends and relatives know.
We had phone numbers, itineraries and maps,
So all would be aware where we go!

Old towers, ruins, castles, and many churches
Were shown brilliantly by **Mike**, our guide.
It's hard to imagine all this information,
Could be shared—(we'll never know if he lied)!

He shared interesting facts about the animal business,
Like, sheep identified by a colored patch.
These sheep and cows were some animals,
That roamed widely, making them hard to catch!

Mike gave such important and clever information,
That we voted to put a star in his crown—
He explained that of all of the deeds done in the world,
The undertaker will be the last to let us down!

One of the most exciting places to visit
Was the Belleek china factory, a guided tour.
We could purchase any pieces and send them home—
What gift could you give any newer?

We were in the North in the Mountains of Mourne.
The short tour of Belfast, was with a local guide, too!
Max and I had a special experience—
Had dinner with Irish children we knew!

The Shores of Galway Bay and Cliffs of Moher
Were so exciting, to say the least—
Yes, extravagant beauty, a phenomenal view—
As God prepared for us, He displayed a feast!

A highlight of interest to us country folk
Was the performance of a Border Collie with sheep.
Training begins at four months with these dogs—
They performed on the side of a mountain, quite steep!

Only 8% of the land is trees, we were told,
Golf courses can be seen quite a lot—
All of this elegance we take so for granted—
We've not a clue what all <u>we've</u> got!

Most gorgeous rainbows we enjoyed,
At a site we could pull over and see—
They were visible about one minute or less!
Some of God's great handiwork—for free!

Kill, bally, kerry, innis and lough
Are common beginnings of words used there.
They have meanings of real Irish culture,
And describe the native expressions in the air!

Flags are displayed in all regions of the land—
Mike shared this very interesting fact—
There are five places where <u>ours</u> is never lowered—
This unusual bit of knowledge, I lacked!—

Arlington Cemetery, Home of Betsy Ross, Pearl Harbor,
The Alamo, and one placed on the moon!
This was a neat bit of history, as we traveled—
I'd have never thought of them all very soon!

Here's some fun-talk by **Michael**, the driver—
Gave facts which turned out quite suiting—
"What goes clippity-clop, bang, bang, clippity clop?"—
It's an Amish drive-by shooting!

We filmed the piebald horses,
As we traveled from green field to green.
These, I call Holstein horses,
Most interesting farm animal I've seen!

We sat long—we needed movement,
So we took advantage of a fitness room call!
Lo! And behold there was **Kate**—
Setting a good example for us all!

Giant's Causeway was a display of handiwork.
It was quite a climb up and back, too.
'Twas wise to stop and regain some wind,
Like many of us older ones must do!

Max and I had an ice cream cone
At Sneem village where we rested.
Two small dogs and one large one was hungry!—
Would Max share his with them?—he was tested!

It was an education, without question,
As we changed our currency into theirs.
This experience was such a blessing for us all,
No event in our life ever compares.

There is much more to say about the tour—
We will try to live our lives more purely—
We'll be aware as we share what we learned—
You'll probably hear lots of "Aye, Surely!"

MICHAEL HOGAN, DRIVER

The American Flag

There are many poems written;
There are many songs sung, too,
About the emblem of our land,
It's our flag, the red, white and blue!

The red stands for blood that was shed,
Making our land free and secure!
The blue is for bravery and loyalty;
White promotes deeds that are pure!

Oh! What beauty, there's no likeness;
We stand with dignity and pride,
As it waves high above others,
As in God, our Maker, we abide!

Retirement

What a life to be retired,
From the "wild" force to earn money,
To this relaxing and carefree attitude—
I've even accused rainy days to be sunny!

Now, I know God's planned all things,
I feel sure He has a plan for me.
He's given me a mind, body, and soul,
I should be busy as I can be!

I must get to the work to be done.—
I think that there's much here to do.
I feel the call to associate
With the ones He wants me to!

I've been advised by my leaders,
To get my homework done first—
Search the scriptures and pray a lot—
These are what's needed the worst!

Now I can set up a schedule,
With Wal-Mart out of my way;
I'll prioritize God, church, and family,
Isn't that what the scriptures say?

I can even witness in Wal-Mart!—
Before, I dare not show a sign
Of any promotion of missions,
Or any personal feeling of mine!

I'll work in our new computer,
Hoping not to abuse any time,
For I know I can be addicted,
And even fall into some crime!

I've a notion to consider greeting cards,
Creating originals, for it does appear
That one needs to be doing this,
For Helen Steiner Rice isn't here!

I've a tiny young granddaughter,
To answer when she asks why,
She's been taught to respect elders—
I can't show perfection, but I'll try!

This poem doesn't have an ending,
But let's stop here for now
And pick up right here later,
And continue as TIME does allow!

House-boat Fun

On a beautiful day in September
We drove north to Rainy Lake.
This is in northern Minnesota,
And a house boat we did take!

For four days on this fun boat,
We learned more than we ever knew!
The aquatic world is so much different
Than traveling the land like we do.

The weather was just excellent—
The temperature was 60, 70, thereabouts,
If this isn't contrary to a normal September,
I seriously have my doubts.

We took plenty of food along,
As this was very well-planned,
For, you see, when there's no exercising,
One's weight gets out of hand.

There were bear, loon, and beaver at work,
We saw eagles and ducks, oh, so many!
They were getting ready for winter,
And our sailing didn't bother them any!

Max and **Kenny** went fishing every day,
Which was one main reason we came.
They caught some—we ate fish—
Their site was never the same!

Due to scarcity of rain in this area,
Water level was down three feet.
We were careful to read the charts—
One must, while in the driver's seat!

The steering seemed slightly difficult,
The helm had just a little "play".
Our drivers got an extra workout,
But they didn't seem to mind it that way.

I have a "thing" about traveling,
It's to know which direction it was;
Very few times did the sun set in the west—
Nor rise where I know it does!

The service and helpers at Rainy Lake
Were super—were really the best!
We enjoyed tremendously our 4-day stay
It's such a joyous way to get a rest!

Section 8.
Special people

This section is of love and laughter,
some sickness, some sadness—
all of these and others
who have played such
an important part of my life.

It is time to "Give thanks to the Lord,
for he is good; his love endures forever.
Psalm 118:1

Alumni Meeting, 1998

'Twas the fifth day of May
Of the year nineteen forty-eight,
Twelve young men and women,
Became graduates on that date!

It was at the school called Metea,
That has since been torn down.
The plot is used another way;
It looks different in that part of town.

I would like to share with you,
Thoughts that are right down cool!
We received all of our education
In that Bethlehem Township school.

There were 9 of the 12 that managed,
To stick together 12 years straight.
Many did come and go, you see,
Because of moving all over the state.

It was just 50 years ago in May,
The 12 of us waved good-bye
To that wonderful structure of incidents,
It's where such sweet memories lie.

We each could probably write a book,
And tell of all the happenings there,
Some are good, some are bad,
Some would probably curl your hair!

I walked down a big, long lane
To the "hack" that waited for us;
I wore long socks and snow pants,
As I waited to get on that bus.

We had teachers we'll never forget—
Mrs. Cotterman taught us first grade,
Then **Miss Mary Rogers**—the second,
Those sweet memories will never fade!

Mary Barrett taught with firmness,
I resisted, but what's the use?—
She paddled me on my birthday—
Today, it's called child abuse!

We were very disciplined in the 5th grade—
Taught by a lady who'd served in the WACS.
Her name was **Miss Edna Roberson**,
Who gave us many important facts!

There were several outstanding teachers,
But I believe **Ruth Johnson** was unique!
She was soft spoken, but sincere,
Her eyes were her communication technique!

Now to Junior High—up stairs we go:
It was a different world of education.
We didn't sit in one seat all day;
We moved in many a rotation!

We went to music, if we chose,
We sat in assembly hall, if not.
We then had a chance to do homework,
Caught up on that, if we forgot!

We had **Catherine Justice** for Home Ec.—
She was so loving and fun.
She brought her new-born to school,
To show us how child-rearing was done!

Orlon Kingery was the janitor;
He lived in a house near the school.
He gave us candy, if we helped with trash!—
We tried to skip class, but he was hard to fool!

Then in high-school we were blest,
We had teachers dedicated to mankind;
The **Valentines** we shall long remember—
More distinguished educators, you'll not find!

Mr. Valentine wore glasses at his desk,
But looked over them to look at his class;
Mrs. Valentine blinked much as she talked,
And said, "Stop laughing or you'll not pass!"

I can remember the little trick she played,
While we were waiting for the bell,
At the second that we'd be dismissed,
She purposely poked her finger parallel—

To the button that would ring the bell loudly,
But, by avoiding it, the bell hadn't sounded,
Half of the students were up and gone,
She ordered them to return or get grounded!

Mrs. Richeson taught us English,
And she took good care of her nails—
I had problems concentrating,
See, priorities in order never fails!

Mr. Oler was a good typing teacher,
But he didn't allow us to chew gum.
I tried to avoid chewing while he was looking,
But he always caught me—he wasn't dumb!

Mrs. Jones was in the music department,
She taught us to make count each minute,
Whoever heard of piano in band—
I only joined, for I knew Max was in it!

Janie Cox was an English teacher;
She taught French—I didn't do bad.
It did me no good for later in life—
I did correspond with a French lad!

Florence Kreigh was a teacher of music,
She enjoyed teaching a great deal.
Her hair was red; she had pretty teeth,
We all wondered if they were real!

We had **Mabel Thommen** and **Ivyl Fultz**—
I can't remember what they taught.
I can see their form in my memory—
Miss Fultz was tall, the other—"shaught".

Mel Ott taught science, I'm told.
I can't remember him at all—
Someone said he was smart and skinny,
And appeared to be not too tall!

JV and **Juanita Zieg** were teachers—
Husband and wife—quite a pair!
He was principal and she taught math,
They neither had patience to spare.

Wilbur Zieg was a principal at Metea,
We remember him as father of **Joan.**
We knew we could get by with much,
As long as she said we can.

Mr. Smith was a principal, too.
He was a popular guy, I'm sure.
He had a great sense of humor,
But lots of problems he did endure!

Russel Fiedler was our senior class sponsor,
He was coach and history teacher, too.
He and **Mary** sponsored our senior trip,
Made sure we had plenty to do!

I don't remember the sights we saw—
The trivial things, I remember well—
Two of the class had cigarettes on the train,
And I promised that I'd never tell.

Those twelve years are fun to remember—
We felt our class was one most outstanding.
Those twelve students set out in the world,
 But found society so demanding!

We are so proud of Metea High School,
 We were educated to face mankind.
It's our greatest desire that underclassmen
 Will do well with what we left behind!

This Is Your Life—mother

For eighty years now
You've had joys and strife.
Let's review some of it now,
Yes, Mother, this is your life.

Your children and grandchildren
Have meant a lot to you.
To reminisce over these
Is what we shall do.

True friends and many relatives
Make one's life complete,
Let's make mention of them,
Some we have here we can greet.

Some children have connections
With different friends we know,
So as we go down the line,
We'll talk of them as we go.

Reverend and **Mrs. Skelton,**
Special minister and wife;
We appreciate your prayers
And support through Mother's life.

A minister who served
As her dear family grew up
Was **Reverend Harry Rea** in Florida;
He helped to overflow her cup.

Lloyd and **Doris Strong**
Have been such close friends.
As far as neighborhood tangles—
They helped all to make amends!

Ed and **Juanita Burk**, please stand
And let us make it known;
You taught her Sunday School class,
And her spiritual life has grown!

A kind and thoughtful neighbor,
Known as daughter number six, that's who!
You see, our parents had five girls,
Lucille Grable was one they claimed, too!

Mrs. John Meents is now eighty,
She lives over across the way.
Her comforting thoughts and visits
Came almost any time of day!

The Sunday School class of Metea
Are a group to recognize.
If awards were given for support,
They would win first prize!

Elaine Clemons came over
When **Betty** would be gone,
She'd entertain Mother—
Stayed sometimes 'til dawn!

Jane and **Carl Rentschler**, were
Good friends and neighbors for years!
They've supplied food and laughter—
Even shared a few tears!

Brenda and **Kevin Mundy**,
Good neighbors close by.—
If you saw her teach **Doug**,
You'd understand why.

June and **Ed Garrow** was first daughter,
She's a lot like her mother.
She's quiet and considerate,
Has patience like no other!

Chris and **Bob** are their offspring;
Their lives have been busy,
Getting a good education,
Making some of us dizzy!

Dick and **Gladys** are the couple
Born next in the family tree.
He served in the Armed Forces;
They had a family of three!

Jim is the oldest grandson—
Two children are from him.
Andrew and **Tara** are their names—
We are glad to see them!

Andrew was born September 11th-
A fact we want to stress—
Born on his Grandma's birthday—
Best day to be born, no less.

Ron and **Pat** from Monticello
Had **Rodney** and **Tanya**, boy and girl!
Salesman is **Ron**'s business,
Giving "machinery parts" a whirl.

Ron is oldest great-grandchild—
Interesting facts to remember—
The other 24 were born another day—
Mother writes them all down to remember!

Rita and **Gene Floor** have
Shannon, **Shawn**, and **Shane**.
Gene drives a semi, Rita's a musician,
And the pumpkin business they maintain!

Harriet Kintner, she used to be,
But that's not her name now.
She's **Harriet Kenworthy**—
Would you please take a bow?

Rachel's from Mishawaka,
Claiming **Jeff** as her son.
He's a lot to talk about—
Too bad there's only one.

She's been at Uniroyal—
For twenty years, it was Ball Band!—
Cake decorating, beautician, and quilting—
Wasted hours could be counted on one hand!

It's been a long time, since
We've seen **Doris** and **Delores Young**.
We welcome sweet memories—
Remember songs they've sung?

Don and **Donna** are from Mexico,
Or Florida, or Bunker Hill.
Their lives have been busy,
And probably always will.

For there's **Mike** and **Deb**
Near Deedsville, farming,
With sons, **Scott** and **Seth**—
Have actions, quite alarming!

Twila and **Dave** are teachers—
Teaching their small two!—
Serena six, and **Nathan** three—
Now teaches a North Miami crew.

Anita and **Gene** are located
At either Martinsville or here,
And little one-year-old **Jacob**,
Is one we hold dear!

Chris and **Scott** have been around,
Stationed in Germany for a while.
Little **Jessica** and her beauty
Has made the rest of us smile!

Mark is the wise one—
Being first in his class;
Now engaged in farming—
As for girls—says, I'll pass!

Larry Sharp has gone to meet Jesus,
But he left **Lori**, his wife—
We also enjoy **Danny**—
He's a good kid for one's life!

Audrey is Lori's girl,
She's not little any more.
May she turn out to be
What God wants her for.

Bill and **Lucile**, from Logansport,
He's been a railroader since eighteen.
He's had major operations—
Now, he's not so mean!

Kathy, their oldest daughter,
Keeps us walking the chalk!
Kenny, railroads like his Dad,
Has recently found a new walk!
(with Jesus, Praise God!)

Mary Jane studied hard
To get a doctor's degree!
Danny Joe is right now deciding,
What he'd like to be!

Dewey and **Ginny** are from Burnettsville,
He's been with central-paving,
Has been a hard-working man—
Therefore, always behaving!

Cindy was a little angel!—
That's how we rate her,
But left when she was ten—
We'll understand later.

Joe Dean went to Purdue—
Good banking, he desires.
Rose Ann goes there, too.—
Wants homemaking 'til she retires.

Lisa starts her college work—
You guessed it—Purdue!—
I'll guess she succeeds—
Would it surprise you?

Nina and **Ray** are dairying—
Yes, I'm the dairy queen,
I enjoy writing poetry, and
Selling Avon in between!

Nancy has her Masters,
A degree in physical education,--
Lives in Kalamazoo, Michigan.—
YMCA is her work station!

Greg and **Jo** have 500 veal calves
And one precious little boy.
Jeremy Ray is their three year old,
Grandma and Grandpa's pride and joy!

Leah and **Mike** live in Fulton,
But to go South are their plans.
They're handy and successful—
Answering to many demands.

Hal is still in school—
Enjoys 4-H and the band,
But when it comes to milking,
He's his Mom's favorite hired hand!

Grandma Warner came today
To join all this fun.
Who's responsible for **Ray Warner**?
This lady is the one.

Nancy's friend **Scott Knowles**
From Ann Arbor, he did arrive.
You can surely see him standing!
Yes, he's about six feet five.

Betty Jean Gerrick
Came and stayed many nights—
Enjoyed Mother's cooking,
Managed the extra bites!

She is now **Betty Parker**,
We'd welcome with open arms;
It would be fun to enjoy,
A bit of her charms.

Betty and **Ed** are on the home place—
Her business has been booming.—
Hair styles, cuts, and shaves,
And she promotes good grooming.

Doug is someone special
For the young or the old.
He's who keeps Grandma going,
He's worth his weight in gold.

The Naughty Bunch is here,
But you could never pick them out;
So when I call your name—
Would you give a little shout?

Grandma Riddle came to join us,
In January, she'll be ninety;
She's family, friend, and companion—
She's small, but she's mighty!

Joan is the youngest—
Lived in Indianapolis, quite a spell;
She's been in accounting business and
Rings Republican headquarter's bell!

Here's a familiar gentleman
For whom we'll make way!
A welcome to **Charles Kingery**
And his wife, **Phyllis**, today.

There's someone here today;
If you don't know her, you should.
Edith Zieg is a long time friend,
She's as friendly as she is good!

Bill and **Millie McGuire**
Are two people we hold dear!
For our game during deer season,
They've cut it, year after year.

Bill has a special relationship
To our family gathering, yes,
He and Uncle **Winnie Wiles**
Did what all boys should confess!

Diane Yost, **Brad Outland**, and
Marlene Hughes are Joan's friends
Always welcomed for these occasions
Whenever she attends.

Cousin Ella, we love you
For being just one of our crowd!
I can be really quiet about it,
I'd like to be really loud!

You make a lot of friends,
When we just turn you loose,
You make a real engine,
And even a great "caboose".

Well, Mother, we're proud
To be one of yours,
For you've been the best helper,
We ever had with our chores.

You've helped us hoe melons—
You've helped us saw wood,
You even shucked corn—
Did everything you could;

So that us kids would grow up
To be Christlike and coherent.
You've set the best example
For us, as a parent!

May God, in His generosity,
Bless you galore,
Shower you with abundance
"Til you can't receive any more!

May we, as your children,
Friends, and neighbors, and other,
Be thoughtful, loving, and Christlike,
Striving to be tops like you, Mother!

Now to you who came today
To make her day complete,
We express appreciation
That's really hard to beat!

If I left out your name,
It wasn't planned that way!
Count yourself a part of us all,
And have a good day!

Mother Graduated Nine

There are ones here to be honored
For one reason or another.
It seems so timely and in order,
That we honor each mother.

The special mother I shall honor
Is a gracious mother of nine.
She's quite a "Mom" for a pattern—
She's that sweet mother of mine!

June was her first-born;
She was quiet in her ways;
But to find as much wisdom—
You'd probably look for days!

She graduated in thirty nine
At the top of the class;
She was never outspoken—
Her wit was of brass!

Richard, the firstborn son—
Dick, is how he's known.
Graduated in nineteen forty one—
Knew exactly where he was goin'!

To the Armed Forces he did go,
And Mother was faithful in writing.—
Waited anxiously for his return—
Letters coming home were exciting.

Rachel was daughter number two;
I could write a book about her!—
She enjoyed hard work—
We could not have lived without her!

She graduated in nineteen forty three—
Worked at Uniroyal for years!
Ran from cake decorating to beauty shop,
Made quilts as she shifted gears!

Don is Mother's second son—
He graduated in forty five,
Skipped school to work at home,
So we all could stay alive!

He, too, went to the service,
Won every battle he fought!—
Made the enemy vanish, at least—
That's always what I thought!

Bill was next in the family—
Was easy for us to pick at!
But he did more mean tricks,
Than you could shake a stick at!

Bill wanted to go to the Army.
But age fifteen was too young;
"How will you know 'til you try?",
Is the song he'd always sung!

He graduated in forty seven!—
For the teachers, it was a treat!
Then was a railroader so faithful—
His wife and family are hard to beat!

Dewey was child number six.
He graduated in forty eight.
His grade card wasn't too bad,
But I'm the one who studied late!

He went to Germany as a soldier;
Mother was proud of him, too!
Then he settled in Burnettsville,
Working hard with a construction crew!

Number seven is a meaningful number,
That's me, did you guess?
Dewey and I graduated together,
We're not twins, I'll confess!

You see, he never failed a grade,
But, together, I took one and two.
It was a little of a challenge,
But not really hard to do!

Betty was next in line,
She graduated six years later—
Was a little shy, and I don't know why—
All little boys wanted to date her!

She didn't do that—she studied,
She did what she was told.
She then became a beauty operator,
And is worth her weight in gold!

Joann graduated in nineteen fifty five,
Mother's last to walk down the lane!
She graduated with honors, and
College entrance she did gain!

She went to Manchester College,
Making Mother and Dad proud,
To have one of our family,
To be applauded very loud!

Isn't it neat that all of us
Graduated from the same school?
Not only is it unusual—
I think it's rather cool!

Mother, you've been super,
To have suffered through all our pains!
We want to have a trait like that,
Yes, one who never complains.

So, at this alumni celebration,
And, too, on Mothers' Day,
May God give His richest blessings
In His unique and special way!

In Memory of Johnnie
(son of Max's Goddaughter)
From Nina

Johnnie, I enjoy remembering
Your ever-present smile!
You never seemed discouraged,
You went an extra mile;

To make sure those around you,
Did not get upset,
By noticing your problem,
You hoped that they'd forget!

I know you're having soccer fun,
Or what you and Jesus decide to do!
I look forward to seeing you again,
Where unbearable pain is through!
In the love of Jesus,
Nina

Happy Anniversary!

You are two special people!
You've been a good pair to imitate!
You work and play together,
Each other you tolerate!

When someone needs your assistance,
You're right there to do it!
You always do it with ease,
Like there's really nothing to it!

You never seem to complain!
You take it all in stride!
If we had your likeness,
We'd have nothing to hide!

In fact, we'd be mighty proud
If we had your get-up-&-go!
If we had what you have,
We'd let the whole world know!

So let me tell you this, folks—
Here is just one clue!—
Your love and devotion to your Lord & family,
Makes us want to be like you!

Happy Anniversary, **Rachel** and **Kenny**!
Love from above, Max and Nina

Rachel

Congratulations and best wishes
For being persistent and loyal,
During those treasured forty years
At Mishawaka's Uniroyal!

You've shared with your family,
Those co-workers from Ball Band.
You never brought home one
We didn't think was grand!

You've gotten up early
And headed down to that place;
Was greeted with challenges,
That weren't all fun to face!

You've been an inspiration
To all your family and friends;
So hard-working and dependable—
Your goodness never ends.

"Catcher" on the ball team,
Was a highlight of great fun!
Who kept up the team spirit?
I'd say, "You're the one!"

The Red Ball magazine
Kept us all up to date—
Some news came quickly,
For some, we did wait!

A basketball team organized
With you as a guard,
I know if you didn't win,
You surely tried hard!

In the early years you worked there,
You made all kinds of boots!
If the style wasn't available,
You came up with substitutes.

You entered the tennis department
In the year of '66.
You surely were a "sole-winner",
By using your "old tricks"!

Foam was being made then,
And you were right in there, too,
Keeping up your end of it
As only you can do!

Flex-lite is the product
You worked with before!
You were handy in that department—
Didn't seem like a chore!

Now, it's lab-work and testing
What all samples contain—
Making sure of good quality—
What will burn or resist stain.

Aside from the factory,
You've made yourself a name!
There was never a dull moment—
"Busy"—the name of your game.

You've been cake-decorating
Which takes some of your time.
You always enjoy it,
If you don't make a dime!

Your beauty shop, an addition—
Number of friends increased,
You've made some ladies beautiful—
Yes, a miracle, to say the least!

For the next 40 years,
May whatever you incur
Be as full of excitement
As these last 40 were!

May the Lord bless your efforts,
As He has already done;
May you gain heavenly wealth
From God's loving Son!

Like Dad always said,
Forty times and then some—
"There's only one **Rachel**—
One now, one in Heaven to come!"

Showers of Blessing, Rachel—80

There shall be showers of blessing,
We'll honor **Rachel** with love.
She has just now turned to be 80,
Her life has been sent from above!

CHORUS:
SHOWERS OF BLESSING,
SHOWERS OF BLESSING WE NEED!
OUR LIVES WOULD ALL BE MUCH BETTER,
FOLLOW **RACHEL**, LET'S LET HER LEAD!

There are many happenings in her life;
We shall reminisce as we sing;
She was the first early riser—
Chores, melons, or just did her thing! (Chorus)

She had lots of fun with her classmates
By bringing them home from school.
She was proud to show off the family,
Did she really stick to a rule? (Chorus)

She followed **June** to Mishawaka;
She went to work at Ball Band—
Put in 43 years, set a record!
Was always giving someone a hand! (Chorus)

She married **Bill Young** at age 20—
Gave birth to **Jeff**, who was her pride;
He became quite like his mother—
She had needs, he was right by her side! (Chorus)

Jeff always brought or sent roses,
For each occasion that ever came by!
Oh! What a sweet blessed mem'ry;
He was surely my kind o' guy! (Chorus)

Jeff became top rank in Boy Scouts;
Enjoyed life –did no one any harm,
Made friends, like **Colonel Dave Parks**,
Drove tractor, helped Uncle **Ray** on the farm!   (Chorus)

Jeff was taken to be with his Master,
Left without warning at all,
This has changed her life completely;
We'll not know before we get the call!   (Chorus)

Forty three was her lucky number—
The year of graduation from school.
Ball Band set on 43 acres—
Worked 43 years there—isn't that cool?!   (Chorus)

She taught me how to write poetry;
Also taught me how to decorate cakes—
Was able to do one really fast—
Was not aware of all my mistakes!   (Chorus)

Rachel played on Ball Band's ball team;
She was catcher, not bad at the bat!
Sister **June**, was on her team, as well,
The rest of us are all proud of that!   (Chorus)

She married **Kenny** and they've been traveling
To every state with their motor home.
They've been places to collect lighthouses,
And a record of where they did roam.   (Chorus)

She always had time for the family,
Went to weddings and all their events—
Graduations or just in a hospital—
Made the effort, whatever the expense!   (Chorus)

One profession was that of beautician!
Shampoos and sets—her delight!
A blessing to all of her customers—
A warm welcome, morning and night!   (Chorus)

Quilting is one of her joy-times,
Cutting patterns of her own;
Stayed up many hours working—
Working her hands to the bone! (Chorus)

When all of us sisters got together,
Meeting at **Joan**'s or wherever fun.
She was the life of the party,
At dawn or the setting of sun! (Chorus)

It's our prayer for your life ahead, **Rachel**,
To have good health in all that you do.
Just remember, we're all here beside you!
Just look around—there's quite a crew!

Written by Nina Lynch, July 2005

Evelyn,

We've had some good times together;
These are times we hold dear,
You and **Fred** kept in touch with us!
We only let a few things interfere!

Our children followed along
With 'most everything that needed done,
Whether it was gardening or fishing,
Or just plain having fun!

We shared gardening habits;
You and Fred worked like crazy!—
Growing onions and getting them sold!—
No one had time to be lazy!

We enjoyed your egg-decorating project;
Many clubs and organizations you entertained!
What talent and beauty you shared,
And I know many friends you gained!

The cabin in the Upper Peninsula,
Is a place where we do recall;
When we went fishing, used fish for supper!—
We fried the fish and ate them all!

This is a fact we also know,
We can listen for an eternity through,
Hearing the guys' many conversations,
About the fun things they had yet to do!

May your birthday, **Evelyn**, be special,
And be filled with what you enjoy a lot!
I'm sure you're going to be the happiest,
Just to visit with all the friends you've got!

Dear friends, since God so loved us we also ought to love one another.
1 John 4:11
April 21, 2003

This was printed in the county newspaper after our mother went to be with the Lord.

We would like to say thank you,
You've all done so much.
You've given time and effort,
You always add the right touch.

The bounteous meals were prepared,
It was food, at its best—
We felt honored to be served,
It's through you, God has blest!

Much food was sent to homes;
Expressions of sympathy were sent.
It's hard to express to you,
How much it all meant!

We appreciate **Bruce** and **Rosemary**,
For the music part of it all.
We're thinking an unsaved person,
Might just answer God's call.

Words spoken by **Reverend Ritchie**
Were so appropriately phrased,
When God's servants are in charge,
We never cease to be amazed.

Woodlawn Center is recipient
Of a very generous amount,
Thanks to you, in Mother's honor,
On friends, we can always count.

The lovely floral arrangements
Were a sight to behold.
To all of you, we say thank you,
You're worth your weight in gold!

May His love surround you,
May you feel His presence, too,
For we know Mother's with Jesus,
Just waiting for me and you!

The children of Goldie Coffing

In Memory of Brother Don

The Lord is my shepherd,
I shall not want or fear!
He maketh me to lie down in green pastures—
Right next to my new John Deere!

One whole book of poetry,
Is what I think I'd be writing,
To tell you all about Don—
Each event, I think, is exciting!
You see, he's that brother of mine,
Who worked hard when he was little!—
In sawing wood, milking cows, or planting corn,
Don was right there in the middle!

He didn't enjoy school days much,
He'd rather be home with Dad!
I think Dad felt the same way,
For Don was about the best to be had!
The John Deere Implement Company,
Had lots of Don's attention!
There were many hours of night-work—
He made good use of this invention!

He was willing and went to the army—
We were so proud when he went to war!
We were all so confused—
We didn't know what he was fighting for!
A young lady at the "Double-Dip" shop—
Was one who Don loved for sure!
She was exactly the right one for him—
And he never stopped loving her!

Their first child was a beautiful little girl,
And I watched as **Twila** grew!
I decided if I ever had children,
I'd appreciate, first, a girl, too!
Mike was the most handsome little guy,
Especially playing high school basketball!
If it's ever a sin to be proud,
This young man was the cause of it all!

Anita arrived to be a sweet little sister—
Filled her life with good management traits!
She's such a fine young teacher,
"Sharp"—is how she rates!
Chris came along as number four—
Presented the family with two lovely girls!
All of these were precious to Don—
Their value is much more than pearls!

Mark is who we'll call number five—
Has wisdom—there's no one to blame it!
Was number one in his class of students—
Can farm or do other work—you name it!
Danny Sofianos is a welcome soul!—
He became part of the family, too!
He helps take care of all of us!—
To police is what he chose to do!

Don & Donna were good examples—
They can be proud of their achievement!
Don was so grateful for these—
It seems so unfair to soon have bereavement!
There'll always be flea markets, I suppose,
But not the same without Don!
He was the master of all sales—
Whether a John Deere or some socks to put on!

He loved his Lord, and was faithful,
Keeping Christ first as his being!
We'll miss his generous sharing,
But, in his children,
That's what we'll be seeing!

The Lord is my shepherd,
I shall not want or fear!
He maketh me to lie down in green pastures—
Right next to my new John Deere!

April 6, 2003

A Loving Tribute to My Brother Bill

The nine of us Coffing children
Grew up and were asked to be still,
But if anyone made any noise,
You can be sure it was brother **Bill**!

We walked the lane to catch the bus,
When the winters had quite a chill.
Guess who carried me many times,
You're right, it was brother **Bill**!

When I learned to play the piano,
Any compliments were quite a thrill.
My family encouraged me a lot,
But I could count on brother **Bill**!

My job, when small, was to shell corn,
For we never went to the mill.
The cattle got fed and I had help!—
You guessed it—'twas brother **Bill**!

Work had to be done in the garden—
We raised food from muskmelon to dill.
I can remember all working diligently,
But I can't remember brother **Bill**!

He had a clever way of disappearing,--
We discussed this at the supper table.
There was always a good explanation—
He explained that he just wasn't able!

That kid got more lickin's
Than all of us ever will—
Dad wanted us all to behave,
But he worked harder on brother **Bill**!

He was eager to go off to war—
He chose not to be ignored!
He signed up at an early age—
Dad explained this at the draft board!

When his wife, **Lucile**, had to go,
He had Christlike independence, too!
He set a good example for the rest—
He seemed always to know what to do!

I always say things I shouldn't,
And, yes, the beans I always spill!
But the one who told it like it was—
You're right, it was brother **Bill**.

Many fun and exciting things happened,
Many pages of a book it would fill,
But there's no doubt that lots of it
Would be centered around brother **Bill**!

Second Corinthians one, three and four
We find words to encourage us now!
We are comforted, so we comfort others,
Bill had a handle on this, somehow!

Written August 10, 2002

Lucile

Lucile has gone to be with the Lord
She really fought a hard fight!
Three months ago she made a request,
For three major events happen,--Right?

First was that their 36-year-old son, **Dan**,
Be baptized, and a new life, found.
This happened and we're all rejoicing—
This made their whole family heaven-bound!

Then her mother was ill with diabetes,
And recently went to her heavenly abode—
This was satisfying for **Lucile**,
For this, too, lifted her load!

Then twin grandchildren came along
To be loved and enjoyed by her!
God knows how to give what is best—
Just knows how to let good things occur!

Lucile then went home, happy—
We'll all miss her a lot,
For she kept peace among many,
Now, we all want to have what she's got!

There was a little girl named **Cindy**—
Her beauty was rare to behold!
She was always willing to share what she had,
But only lived 'til she was ten years old.

All the family sadly miss her—
Nothing has been the same without her!
She had made it known she loved Jesus;
There was never anyone who would doubt her!

Her voice seemed to stand out among many,
Even her family and cousins will say—
She was known to be quite the peacemaker,
She's remembered with that trait to this day!

Virginia, Dewey, Rosann, Lisa,
And **Joe Dean**, are those of her very own.
Then, we who make up the ones that she left,
Have experienced more grief than we've known.

When Mothers and Daughters Are Friends

When mothers and daughters are caring and close,
They bring so much joy to each other,
They listen with love,
They speak from the heart,
They're more than just daughter and mother.

Their lives are enriched in such beautiful ways,
And the warmth of their closeness extends,
Beyond their relationship
And into the gladness
Of sharing and caring friends.

(Scrub-buds for a friend)
Some kitchen chores are quite a task—
It's a chore to get something to fight 'em!
Here is the answer to that problem—
Get the job done with this item!

To the Families of Dedicated Volunteers

There's a cross for each of our loved ones,
As we wait, hoping to hear
That all is well, and freedom is won,
We're praying that that time is near!

We seem to be praying without ceasing—
As the Lord has asked us to do;
Urge us, Lord, to help carry crosses
Of those who are dedicated to you!

Our hearts go out to our president,
And those in leadership, high;
A cross that cannot be weighed—
To explain it, we can't even try!

For the volunteering of each man and woman,
We are thankful, each passing day,
As they go abroad to the unknown—
They are praying for our freedom this way!

From Our House (Warner's)
To Your House (Clemons')

You've been our good neighbors;
We've done many things together
When we needed help, you came,
At the drop of a feather!
Our kids grew up together—
All worked like crazy!
There were many cows to milk—
No one had time to be lazy!
Being in the dairy business,
You couldn't get too far away!
You stayed close to home—
Did your "going" some other day!
You two were excellent baby-sitters—
Our kids loved to stay with you!
It seemed like home to them—
They enjoyed all you do!
Anna, I'll always remember visiting you,
Or call to borrow jars or lids,
You took valuable clean-up time,
To sit down and read to your kids!
The event of the century took place,
When Ray went home to his Master!
You and others made sure,
Our planting time was not a disaster!
You brought in neighbors and equipment,
To get the corn planted that May!
Who would have ever thought,
It could all be done in one day?
May your married life of 50 years,
Be fun-memories beyond measure!
From, when we went to Wisconsin Dells,
To, all the other times we treasure!

Donna and Jerry, 50th

You have been together fifty years!
You're saying, "How time flies!"
You've been good partners for each other;
You solve them when problems arise!

You've gone through trials and temptations;
You've had some of those now and then;
You've taken each other by the hand;
Then hard times were taken with a grin!

The church people look to you
For answers to problems there!
We're blest to have godly people
For guidance, you two use prayer!

We love your gentle spirit;
We know happiness when you're around!
You've a sense of compassion and tolerance;
Its likeness is hard to be found!

We love your participation in Sunday School,
We love what comes from you!
It's always with reassurance and thoughtfulness,
For you share something you've been through!

The music part of our worship
Is enhanced with your taking part!
It's never fake at all with you two;
It's always straight from the heart!

Your children have made you proud,
By serving their Master and Lord!
Their lives have influenced others, too,
Claiming God's Word as their sword!

May you two enjoy good health,
May you enjoy happiness beyond measure!
May the gifts from God's hand of love,
Be those you'll always treasure!

Donna and Jerry Williams—March 2006

Time On My Hands

What do you do with TIME on your hands?
Write some poetry is what I shall do.
Here we are—just Max and me—
On Sunday with Dark Lake in view.

Having two weeks off from Wal-Mart,
We chose a lovely time in September,
To do some repairs and winterize this cabin—
The fun time, we shall long remember!

Before we left home, we started New Image,
To encourage weight loss and better health,
So we really haven't indulged in fat food.
Good health is one form of wealth!

The temperature has been ideal daily—
Not cold, not hot, but just right!
We enjoyed walking three miles a day—
We didn't tire like we thought we might!

The evergreens stand tall in their beauty!
God is changing the colors of the trees!
He's doing it before our very eyes;
It seems it's us He's trying to please!

Max got the television going today—
Football between Minnesota and the Bears.
Minnesota did win the game, you know;
Don't they know how much this fan cares?

We kept in touch with all of our children;
We know **Erika** is changing so fast!
She was hard to leave and say good-bye to—
That kiss and hug just didn't last!

Greg and **Jo** had calves to be sold—
We never miss that event,
But we didn't get to help this time—
Without us—that day just came and went!

Max and I planned each morning to walk—
Together, but never alone.
This time together was special—
We got to "kill two birds with one stone"—

You see, it gets to be rather boring—
Walking alone for three miles—I worry,
Feeling some animal may attack me—
Then, together, time goes past in a hurry.

Traveling home, we had time for shopping;
To get a Holiday Barbie was our goal.
A sales lady at Toys R Us,
Said, "Try Target", God love her soul!

Target had a huge supply—
'Twas Thursday around 10:00 or about;
Since there was one per customer allowed,
By Saturday, they'd probably be out!

Nancy wanted to make sure we enjoyed it—
For safety and good weather, she prayed.
Hal, Greg, Jo, and **Jeremy** made hay—
Rain stopped 'til the hay was made!

I really have a confession to make,
And I'm sure you've gathered by now—
My heart doesn't leave and get away from it all—
I must stay on the farm, somehow!

James came up for the last few days,
To go fishing and get away from sin,
And to help his Dad get the cabin winterized,
For that job was more for two men!

He went fishing a few times;
Didn't catch anything we could label
As ideal for the time we should bother
To supply any food for the table!

There was a relative across the lake—
Uncle **Albert** and brother **Paul** lived there.
There were no women in their lives;
They had this home together to share.

Paul had died and left **Albert** alone—
He says 1911 is when he was born.
This situation needs prayer a lot
The air all around is forlorn!

Those ten days in Minnesota
Were what we needed—we had fun!
God is revealing to us His intentions,
To use His own to get His work done!

I count this all such a blessing—
Our joy cannot be measured,
Except for not seeing **Erika**,
This trip will long be treasured!
Max and Nina 2002

Sailing at Dark Lake, Minnesota

Indiana Extension Homemakers

Indiana Extension Homemakers,
An organization in which many take part,
Is where many find educated assistance,
And enjoy homemaking and many an art!

The North Miami Modern Mrs,
Was a group where I began.
These clubs "bloom" and then vanish;
One cannot make an extended plan.

So, leaving **Nancy Sarver**,
Also **Shari** and **Bonnie Burns**,
Then **Kay Fisher** and **Joan Hart**;
Many lessons one learns;

To keep up with changes,
Many times is hard to do.
Shirley Murphy and **Miriam Butler**,
Were a part of our crew!

I went to Allen Township,
To join the ladies there.
Ann Hattery encouraged me;
Joan Hart's talents are rare!

Katrina Benge and **Becky Smith**,
Then **Norma Warner** and **Betty Routt**,
All shared positive thinking
Of what homemaking is all about!

Adelene Flenner is always faithful.
Donna Halterman is good at leading;
Lana Kuhn and **Kathryn Jones**
Have the talent we are needing!

Bonnie Stout is most recent
To join us with talent she shares.
We are open to new members;
Come singly or in pairs!

Miscellaneous Inserts

You may need a stamp now and then
To pay a bill or send a card.
When the price changes, add 2 cents,
Which shouldn't be very hard!
(Enclosed find a book of stamps)

I knew I could count on you!
You did it so very well!
You do it like you love the Lord—
That fact is so easy to tell!

Willie—We felt really honored
When you took us for that ride,
Into roundabouts and tiny passes,
And up and down the mountainside.
We could never have found the site,
Except for searching for days—
You set a perfect example,
How you Irishmen share your ways.
We really love your family,
We'd like the best for you.
May God bless your efforts
In all you share and do!
We'd like you to come to our land
And see what makes us tick,
And as fast as you comprehend things
You'd do it all pretty quick!

Lou Ann—it's time to celebrate again,
We'd like happiness for you!
Just hope you enjoy life
In everything you do!

Whether you're in big Texas,
Or at home in our state,
I want you to have this greeting—
I don't want it to be late!

This certificate of attendance
Is presented especially for you!
You've been interested and faithful
In the many things we do!
We are praying as you grow,
You'll be serving Jesus more,
And you'll be reaching out to others,
Even more than before!

This certificate of leadership
Is printed especially for you!
You've been attentive and interested
In what our own people do!

We're praying for God's blessing
On your life as you grow
In His grace and dependence
On Him where you go!

Leah—We wish you a happy birthday
With lots of surprises,
Here're lots of hugs and kisses—
They come in all sizes! Love, Max & Mom

Gladys—We said a prayer
For comfort and peace,
"Til you're back to normal
And all pain will cease!
They worked on your hand,
So I know you have pain.
It's amazing what they do
To make them work again!
We love you—Max & Nina

*Psalm 9:11 Sing praises to the Lord
enthroned in Zion; proclaim among
the nations what He has done!*

Kenny, for fixing my car:

You folks have been super—
You've lightened my load,
You've given of your talents,
To keep me on the road!

Money cannot buy
The satisfaction of knowing,
That a faulty car
Won't keep me from going!

May the Lord touch your system—
May God bless you galore!
May good health and wealth,
Be yours and much more!

Shirley, it's fun to have my hairdresser
Live across the street from me.
I shouldn't be late for my appointment,
Being retired, wouldn't you agree?

She does it well, just like I want it,
We talk about what needs to be said!
She's quite the computer gal, too!
I like what she puts IN my head!

Darlene, if I ever had a best friend,
I'd say it would be you.—
You like the things that I like,
And most of what I do!

You see, I can call you
At any time of day
And tell you what I'm thinking
And it's always been o. k.

You don't blurt out to others
The things that really bother,
You just keep it to yourself
And seek our heavenly Father!

So keep on being you, **Darlene**,
For it's on you I can depend,
I'll probably keep looking to you
As my very best friend!

Lana, you and **Larry** are sweet hosts,
You give, and give, and give!,
May God bless you and your family,
As long as you both shall live!

Ed, we're here enjoying the South,
And we're having lots of fun,
But not too busy to send you
Happy wishes from under THIS sun!

May your day be exciting—
These are wishes from Nina and Max,
We hope you'll try to take time to
Just slow down and relax!

I was checking on those
Who are present today and alas!
YOU were not here, smiling,
In my Sunday School class!
We missed you!

Yes, we really miss you,
So please don't stay away,
Just let us know how you're feeling,
Let's stay in touch—O. K.?

May your flight be very enjoyable!
May your arrival be exciting for you!
Just give our love to your family,
We'd really like to be there, too!

May your life be filled with happiness,
May good health be yours, too!
But you have such good parents—
They'll make sure of that for you!

Please get well, **Doug!**
I feel sad when you feel bad,
I don't want you to be sick or down!
Just kick up your heels real quicklike—
Don't let that face wear a frown!
Love, from Aunt Nina

Hanna, we hope this is exciting,
As you start your college career!
It's our prayer you'll enjoy it,
We'll all miss you around here!
Love, from Max & Nina

Julie and Jeremy,
We wish you happiness
As you plan the big day!
For you!—goodness and prosperity,
That's how we pray!
Love, Grandma & Max

Jo and **Greg**
We're wanting you to be warm,
As you go to hunt in the west,
These jackets came from L&M—
We think they are the best!

This may be a little early,
But you can enjoy them more!
Hope they're the right size,
Or they can be exchanged at <u>that</u>
store!

Jeremy, this gift card from Cabelas
Can be used on whatever you desire,
Perhaps some clothes or a backpack,
Or binoculars you might require!

May your birthday be happy—
This is better sooner than later,
Have fun hunting with your Dad—
There's really no hunter greater!

Alec—this money is for your college
Or for whatever you choose to do!
We pray for a life of happiness—
Enjoy what's best for you!
Love, Gr Grandma and Gr Grandpa

Erika—We're sending you money,
To be applied to education,
May you be happy as you grow!—
You're spectacular in every situation.
We love you! Grandpa and Grandma

Barb—The children sang beautifully—
It was because of you!—
Thanks for helping me train them,
To praise the Master, too!

We're sending you a prayer,
You'll have comfort and peace today.
May the good news of healing,
Come to you today!

I like the way you see things,
You've "seen" a way to get well!
With that persistence, I am sure,
You'll be o. k. soon, I can tell!

Jeremy, You're Tops

We're proud of you, **Jeremy**!
To us, you're the best
In making good decisions,
You really pass the test!

The world needs men like you;
You show dignity and pride!
You've been persevering,
You've been right by our side!

When it comes to being a gentleman,
You really top them all!
We know we can count on you,
You're at our beck and call!

Jacqueline

You are a talented young lady!—
So, can you figure this out?—
Just unscramble these words below—
You'll get the message, no doubt!
pypaH dritBhay, quelinJcea

Take your medicine,
Like a good patient should!—
We'd take it for you,
If it would do any good!
(Please get well!)

Alec—May the Lord bless you,
As you follow His ways,
May your steps be easy,
For a million more days!
Love, from Great Grandma and
Great Grandpa

Julie—We wish you happiness,
We wish success for you!—
May you enjoy doing
What you want to do!

I Love You, **Erika**

No card says it all,
But this one comes near—
You are so special, Erika
You're such a little dear!

I had a feeling before
That you'd be pretty and sweet,
But you even top that—
You just can't be beat!
Love in Jesus, Grandma

Donna and **Ray**

It was surely a fun time
To spend a day with you!
You two seem so humble,
Caring for people like you do!

Max and I feel blest,
Hoping to do it again.
May the Lord touch your lives,
And your efforts be not in vain!
In His Love,   Max & Nina

Happy Birthday, **Ed**
I'm not at home, **Ed**,
To make you a birthday card,
But this is even better—
It won't be very hard!

We are here at Florida Keys,
We're having a lot of fun,
But here's a Happy Birthday wish
With a bunch of Island sun!

Stephanie

It's exciting to us
For you to be ten!—
Have fun and be happy,
'Til who knows when!
Love from above, Max & Nina

(cash for a baby shower for **Emilee**)
Ann, you and **Emilee** can go shopping,
And get some things you lack—
Most ladies do enjoy this—
If it's some jewelry or a "Big Mac"!
Enjoy! Love in Jesus,   Leah and Nina

Sympathy
May showers of blessings
Surround you with love;
May the Lord, in His watchfulness,
Send you happiness from above!
Love from above, Max & Nina

To **Mary Ruth**

You play and accompany us well,
That the choir sings the right notes,
So here's a token of appreciation—
The count says you get all the votes!
Merry Christmas!

Song-leader, **Donna**

You've blest us with your talent;
You've led us to sing low and high;
So here's a token of thanks from us—
May you enjoy whatever you buy!
In Jesus' love,   The Choir

Celebrating the 140ᵗʰ Anniversary Of the Mexico Baptist Church

We celebrate and praise God today
For His creation and all He has done!
As a church we are bound together
To give thanks to Jesus, His Son!

Time for Family Fun

Dear **Cousin Esther,**
We sisters came to share with you—
Just loving thoughts we bring.
God has blest us with this privilege,
To do this once-a-year thing!
Enjoy these goodies,
From the Famous Five

Joan, you are the sweetest hostess,
When we come at night to stay—
Enjoy good health, and what's best in life,
Much joy for you, we pray!

June, this Greetings Workshop software,
I chose with great delight:
If you already have this one,
We'll exchange it for one that's right!

Rachel, hope you still enjoy lighthouses,
It was fun to shop for these.
They're such a popular item,
Makes shopping quite a breeze!

Betty, I hope you still enjoy birdhouses,
This mat is for you to use;
You can hang it, or walk on it,
It's for whatever you choose!

Being women of God makes one humble;
Being women of God makes one strong;
For the strength comes from our Maker—
His spirit shows us right from wrong!

You women of God who are mothers,
Hold the highest position on earth!
You children rise up—call her blessed,
Being taught this from their birth!

Women of God carry the news,
To the mission fields, home and abroad.—
Many of their great sacrifices
To many people, may seem odd.

But these women recognize the call,
When a need at hand should be met;
Never counting the cost that's involved—
These women—we'll not forget!

Let's be challenged to be women of God—
Not at ease 'til His work is done.
Be aware to stamp out indifference,
Right up 'til the last soul is won!

He will teach us His ways, so that we will walk in His paths. Isaiah 2:3

Dear **Jo**,
I took a look in Circus World—
More cards than you ever saw!—
I wanted to find the one that said,
"Happy Mother's Day to my daughter-in-law!"
There was none, so I said to myself,
"Self, write your owns words to fit".
So I'll try to say what I want to say,
And not "hem-haw" a bit!
You're the sweetest mother for my grandson,
I'm as pleased as "all-get-out"—
I'm so proud of all you do—

It makes me want to shout!
So have a Happy Mother's Day,
May you relax, let Greg be your host;
Put your feet up, take a nap, or
Do what YOU like to do most!
Happy Mother's Day, from Mom

Donna E. (our director)
We want to say thank you,
This cash may help do it!—
You make it look easy, like
There's really nothing to it!
Merry Christmas, from the choir!

Jeremy, I'm saying a little prayer,
May the time go fast for you!
May the Lord stay by your side
As you do what you must do!
(on vacation)
It's hard to sit and do nothing.
I should put my thoughts in verse.
This could be a poem in my book!

Erika said, "Write about me",
I told her I thought I could!—
She's been an excellent vacationer—
Doing what I didn't think she would!
She plays a lot by herself,
Leaving everyone else be.
Or she suggests we play dominoes—
On that we all did agree!

Allison and Ryan

We wish you happiness,
Long after the cake—
May the joys you encounter,
Be as much as you can take!

Jo and Greg

Congratulations on your new adventure,
May your veal business keep growing!
You've been good examples of progress—
It's time the whole world is knowing!

In the name of our Great Maker

A Father's Day Wish for You, Greg—

There'll be much celebration,
But after all's said and done,
One of the greatest living fathers,
Is the father of my grandson!
Love in Jesus, Mom

Jeremy, you've responded to good training,
You've achieved so much, we're proud!
We think you're the greatest—
We'd like to shout it, loud!

And tell the world who's coming,
Who shall set a striking pace!
You've shown leadership abilities
At every time and place.

Along with your thrusting efforts,
Greater parents,--there are none,
Who encouraged you with godliness
And persistence to get things done!

May the Lord in His great goodness,
Keep blessing and challenging you.
May you let Him be your companion,
'Til you accomplish what you want to do!
In Jesus' love, Grandma and Max

Leah, it's fun to be your mother,
You were beautiful to behold,
Even as a tiny baby,
'Til you've grown to be this old!

Your voice is what I love to hear,
When you call me on the phone,
Or when we can sit side by side,
And chat when we're alone!

I'd like your day to be special;
I want you to enjoy all day.
May your birthday be exciting,
For you deserve it that way!

May God bless your birthday,
From the minute your eyes are open,
'Til reclining time and all is well,
And you've received all you were hopin'!
In Jesus' love, Mom

Time out, **Tyler**,
Hope you have a lot of fun
On your birthday this year!
Yes, we're rooting for you,
With a great big cheer
GOOOO, Tyler, Slam—Dunk!

For **Jaime**

Here's a little angel,
Flying to you, late,
Hoping to get to the party,
In time to help celebrate!
You are eighteen, now, Jaime,
It can't really be true!—
You're a grown lady, now,
And we wish life's best for you!
In Jesus' love, Max & Grandma

Leah—These gifts are from Wal-Mart,
(Who are there to please)—
I'll be glad to exchange them,
If you get duplicates of these!
Love, Mom

Leah—Congratulations and best wishes,
May her arrival be fast!—
I'm so excited—I shall have a blast!
Love, Mom
(before **Erika** was born)

Erika, we're having a birthday party,
Will you come to be our guest?
It's in honor of a friend,
Who is Jesus—He's the best!

Come to Grandpa and Grandma's
On the 23rd of December—
We'll call you on the phone,
So you'll be sure to remember!

Santa has been waiting—
He wants to be here, too!
So make out your list—
It's what he wants you to do!
Love in Jesus, from Gr and Gr

Father, we bow in gratitude,
For the showers of blessings you send!
We are so abundantly supplied—
As on you we solely depend!
You have blest us as a nation,
We are blest beyond compare!
May we show our thanks to you,
And win lost souls?—is our prayer.
Joyfully we give of our abundance,
For this, you asked us to do—
Yes, lovingly, not begrudgingly—
Lord, we really want to lift YOU!
We thank You for life's blessings,
We thank You for all that You've done;
More than anything else, Lord,
Thanks for sacrificing Your Son!
We give You praise, in His name. Amen

Seth, your parents must be mighty proud
To have a son like you,
And you have done, like them,
The things you like to do.

You've been a whiz scholastically,
You've achieved as high as you can.
We're glad to even know you,
Much less, be a part of your clan!

May God bless you as you go farther—
May He be your companion and guide.
He's promised never to leave you,
If you stick close to His side!

So here's a token of our love—
May it help in some small way
To get what you like and need!
Enjoy your future—come what may!
We love you, Great Aunt Nina and Max

Cindy—we wish you joy and happiness
In what you choose to do!
You are in our prayers right now—
We're asking the best for You!
In Jesus' love, Max & Nina

To **Bill Starks**:
I have been so busy,
With so many things to do,
That I completely have forgotten,
To send a note to you!
The cake boards have me spoiled,
They come in so handy!
They are ideal in sizes,
Satisfy cake-lovers just dandy!
For, you see, they are sturdy—
Don't fold like cardboard does,
Was I needing this convenience?—
You bet I really was!
You were so kind and thoughtful,
To do all of these for me—
I know it took some time,
To have them cut so carefully!
It has been my request, you see,
For them to be returned,
But people fail to do this,
Is what I've sadly learned.
I've suggested when they order,
To order a size my boards will fit,
Works out fantastically,
And they don't mind a bit!
Thank you so much—Nina

Mike—it's really fun to reminisce—
It doesn't do any harm
To talk about the earlier days,
When back on the farm!

We worked very hard
To get all the work done.
Good food and good weather
Made it seem like fun!

These thoughts are for you, **Mike**
We hope you enjoy your day,
Just sit back and enjoy it—
Glad you're not making hay!
Happy Birthday, from Nina

Lovera, we greeted at the door,
When we saw there was none!
Yet, it's our job description
To make sure it's done!
You're such a wonderful person,
To stand by and help out,
True love from a friend,
Is what life's all about!

To my **Secret Sister** at Wal-Mart:
I think of you often,
For I have TIME ON MY HANDS!
Hope you're enjoying this weather,
May you manage its demands!
May you keep well and warm—
Travel safely through the snow,
Going to and from work,
And wherever you must go!
Much love!

For a loss of Someone Dear—
To **Donna Jean** and **"George"**
When our friends are sad,
We are really sad, too,
May this little card help
To take the sadness from you!
Love in Jesus, from Max & Nina

Donna—We want to help celebrate,
We want to do it in style,
Here's some cake to do it with—
Put on your biggest smile!
In Jesus' love, from Max & Nina

E-mail Birthday message to **Cindy**—
Here's lots of HUGS—
Do you know why?
They're for your birthday,
That I just let slip by! Love, Nina

Bill Collector

There was an old woman,
Who lived near Peru;
She had so many bills,
She didn't know what to do!
She said to herself,
"Which first shall I pay?"
She sorted them out—
"I'll pay THESE today".
The light bill, the phone bill,
And the groceries were plenty,
Uncle Sam wanted tax money;
He can't wait, can he?
Down at the department store,
She had used her charge plate.
She MUST pay this monthly,
And they don't like to wait!
The local appliance store brought her a TV.
There was a payment on that;
You don't get those free!
After much consideration and pondering a lot,
A big fat hospital bill is one she forgot!
Now if you ask me what I think of this—
The doctor and hospital,
She really shouldn't miss!
Were it not for the efforts
Of those who made her well,
She may have had an added bill—
The mortuary—you can't tell!
Let's pay first things first,
Send your balance right away!
You will be in good standing,
Should you need us another day!

To the von Hartens—July, 2001

It was in the year of '96, that you
von Hartens became a part of our system,
We've been blest by many of your efforts,
It would be so very hard to list 'em!

The weekend that Max and I were married,
Pastor Davis was unable to do it;
There was an emergency in his community,
So, **Mardy**, you came and helped us thro' it!

When **Cecil** fell off the roof last week,
You came to the hospital to pray—
We'll miss your faithful service,
Or, do all ministers serve this way?

You've been a God-fearing minister, **Mardy**,
And that's the kind we need—
You've been one who tells it like it is—
You've really planted good seed!

You've been a good prayer warrior—
You've asked God that we would be, too!
You've accepted us unconditionally—
You've shared "grace" like Jesus would do!

You've promoted visitation—
Encouraged us to help "bring them in"!
You've set a good example—
Your goal has been—souls to win!

You showed patience when **Eileen** grew ill,
You helped her to give us a smile.
You attended to her and kept her
comfortable,
You did it to the very last mile!

You shared your talent of music—
You promoted choir and specials, as well.
You praised us and forgave all our errors—
There were plenty—I'm sure you could tell!

You've been a good father to **Peter**,
See?—he hasn't turned out so bad!
It's so few and far between,
For a kid to have a good Dad!

We are proud to have had you these years,
We feel more Christlike, too!
It has been because of good leadership,
So carefully exemplified by you!

Here, we express our appreciation
From the very bottom of our hearts.
We pray for you God's richest blessings,
We know prayer is where it starts!

We pray for peace and happiness, too,
As you start life with **Peg** and the girls,
We pray, too, your ministry keeps growing,
As the ribbon of His holiness unfurls!

We want to keep in touch with you;
We'll need your prayers, still every day.
Together we're yet under His supervision,
As we stay beside the Master all the way!

Promoting Sunday School attendance

We enjoy your presence,
When you can be here!
We're looking forward—
To the next time you appear!
Miss you!
In Jesus' love—Your Sunday School class
at Mexico Baptist

We get really excited
When you can be here!
We're looking forward to
The next time you appear!
Miss you!
In Jesus' love—Your Sunday School class

All of us are handicapped,
In one way or another,
If it's not a physical appearance,
We may find fault with a brother.
Let's all be determined,
During this season of the year,
To extend more consideration,
To all far and near!
The God who performs miracles,
Is as capable as ever,
To heal bodies, souls, and minds—
Would He forget us?   Never!
So may we all be dedicated
To be renewed this season,
With the healing in God's hand,
Knowing Jesus is the reason!

Wedding in Pennsylvania (Peggy and Mardy von Harten)

"Is there anything we can do for you, **Mardy**?"
Are the words Max so willingly said,
Concerning items to be moved to their home,
Before the day he and **Peggy** were wed.

"Oh, yes, please bring the vacuum cleaner,
And the mandolin—I can't leave it here!
Then there were a few odds and ends—
My mind hasn't been too clear!

Oh, would you mind bringing our dog, **Punky**?—
She rides in a car so well!
She eats and drinks so sparingly,
And her manners, you'll be able to tell!"

She was a good companion—
She just was no trouble at all—
I never thought that an animal
Would be so easy to haul!

We did the ten-hour drive—
It didn't seem that far.
We planned to be there in one day—
Motel reservations for a dog was bizarre!

It was a small beautiful wedding in New York,
The church near Chaffee was small.
Peg had attended here earlier—
The surrounding foliage seemed like fall!

Peg's 14-year-old daughter, **Allison**,
Sang, "Your Love", then vows, they'd say!
Adrien, her 16-year-old daughter, was
Maid-of-honor for this special day!

Peter was in the wedding party—
He took his place with the rest—
All of the family was proud of him—
He looked and did his best!

Mardy's brother, **Carl**, was best man—
A friend, **Dan**, played the organ and sang, too.
Mardy's father was in attendance, also—
(His life in Hawaii seems in view!)

The reception was in the American Legion Post,
In Aurora, just a few miles prior.
The fellowship was friendly, dinner was served,
Then dancing, if you so desire!

We wished them well, then on to Niagara Falls,
Since we were close, we had that planned.
It was such a joy to see God's beauty,
And the power of His mighty hand!

We didn't hurry, for we knew it was impossible,
To get back for church services here,
So we attended the Chaffee Baptist Church,
The minister explained salvation quite clear!

We enjoy traveling and seeing the sights,
But it's always good to be home!
Yes, I enjoy all the exciting things in life—
Gives me an excuse to write a poem!

If You knew Susie Like I Know Susie

Let's sit back and think
Of some things of the past;
Things we enjoy—
Things that will last!

This past summer
Has been a busy one.
Some have had trials,
And, too, we've had fun.

The working and slaving
Of each and every member,
Will be sure to pay off,
But may take 'til December.

The County Fair was a project
That we each had a part;
Not always do we
Put in our whole heart.

But I'm only speaking
For myself alone—
I'm not one to complain
Or let out a groan.

For the projects I entered,
Looked pretty good to me—
I offered the judge glasses
So she could see!

There's one gal among us—
And this is how you'll find it—
She presented her project
With a lot of work behind it!

Not in a big hurry
Did she do her thing,
For her stitching was careful—
Sewing, fit for a King.

Speaking of royalty
From styles I have seen,
This gal, **Susie**
Looked like a Queen!

I watched her model
And she did so with pride.
As the judge called her Champion,
She nearly burst out and cried!

I was really proud of her,
To think I even knew her,
Susie's a champion in character;
Couldn't say anything truer!

She accepted her trophy
With humility and surprise;
The happiness for her family,
Could be seen in her eyes.

A trip to the State Fair,
For her was a thrill;
Just to represent her county,
And to be competing still.

But, can't you see **Susie**,
Standing there looking pretty,
When all of a sudden,
The winner was number thirty!

Susie steps forward,
She just couldn't believe it!—
She stopped her knees knocking,
Long enough to receive it!

We can't really express
What we'd really like to—
We want you to know, **Susie**,
We're sure proud of you!

State Hairdresser Finals
September, 1956

To become an operator,
You must go take a test.
This will prove to everyone,
You can be one of the best!

Betty is a smooth operator—
She used some psychology!
She goes to sister Nina, saying,
"Please accept my apology,

But I need a model,
For the test I must take.
I need someone in need
Of a big difference I can make"

Well, I was desperate to be pretty,
So I accepted her invitation!
Indianapolis—there we went,
To make me a new creation!

I was cautioned not to speak,
Through this tense and important ordeal.
It would count against her passing,
If an error I'd reveal!

So I kept my mouth shut,
As **Betty** set to work.
Once in a while she whispers,
"Nina, please don't jerk".

I even got a manicure,
A "once in a lifetime" pleasure,
Got the facial, too, you see,
Got beauty in full measure!

Well, during the setting of the hair,
Betty's careful, can't you just se'er?—
Fastening hair clips well in place,
She catches one in my ear!

I remember to say nothing,
For she never would have passed!
(This was my first State final,
Also it was my last!)

I used motions, facial expressions,
Acting so much like a mute,
'Til finally that judge looked elsewhere,
As the pain was acute!

Betty DID notice my problem,
She rearranged the clip,
And for the rest of the day,
I had a stiff upper lip!

We've had fun about it;
It really wasn't so bad!
I felt it was an honor
To be of help; I was glad!

May I give this one suggestion,
If an operator you want to be?
Get you a model with lots of resistance—
It'll be less painful,
You'll have to agree!

At The Beauty Shop

For twenty years it has been now
Since **Betty**'s business has been "hair".
She's really worked hard at it—
For each customer, she does care.

She's spent many hours—
Many wee ones in the morning
To keep up her business to satisfy customers—
Many times, has hardly a warning.

Her beauty shop has been a fun-place—
One that proves entertaining.
There were rare and clever demonstrations—
And there's a place of complaining.

It's a place where you find out the facts,
If you really want to know what they are—
A place where you get top information.
It beats radio and TV by far!

You can locate a lost animal, even,
Or pour out your heart, be consoled,
And listen out from under the dryer
To a story someone else has told!

It's a place to find new recipes.
Someone always has a new one going.
You're sure to find out about the neighbor's kids—
Find out what yards they're mowing!

There's a few minutes you can write a letter,
Or just relax—it's your only chance
To figure out your day's work schedule
To wash windows or set out plants.

You can just get beautiful by **Betty**—
That's her prime interest, you know.
It's a place to get all spruced up,
If you have a "dress-up" place to go!

If you need a reason to get in on the fun,
Maybe you don't want to get a style.
Maybe you never get permanents,
But you can get a hair cut once in a while.

There's been soliciting going on in her shop,
Maybe she wasn't even aware of it.
There have been Grandmas who brag on
their grandchildren,
To share in this, we all love it!

For twenty years now, **Betty**'s weathered it,
And I expect she'll go twenty more,
At least we hope and pray so—
May the Lord bless her efforts, galore!

(**Marge** asked for my help
to write a poem about their pet dog. Here it is:)

Let me share our story with you,
It's one of love beyond measure!
Of all the sweet memories we've ever had,
This one we shall always treasure!

Dan is the father of **Ann**, we call "Sis",
"Baby Doll" is our dog who arrived so small!
After thriving with love and adoration,
She never has seemed small at all!

"Baby Doll"
(I lead a dog's life)

My lord and master's name is **Dan**,
But my human little sis is **Ann**,
Who was the first to hold me in her hand.
She tried to tell her Dad how pretty I was, you'll see,
But he wouldn't listen, so she took a picture of me,
You're right, homeward bound were we!

Way back then, I weighed 6 pounds
and now I weigh 60, I'm told,
I am fourteen months old and very hard to hold.
I chase down my toy and say, "Let's play",
As my master tries to read the paper
at the end of the day!

Marjorie Lynch, July 22, 2005

"Strive to Live a Christian Life"
(Summary of the Sermon on the Mount)

When Jesus gave the greatest speech,
Called the "Sermon on the Mount",
He had and spoke with authority—
On this, we surely can count!

For it's the message from His Father—
It's hope for the world to know!
If we take seriously this teaching,
It is sure our faith will grow!

Think how blest we are,
Identifying with each beatitude—
Poor in spirit, meek, and merciful,
No matter what our mood!

Salt and light are powerful substances,
They are so basic for mankind—
A necessity for our earthly lives,
More than any products you'll find!

Keep the law made by government;
Jesus promotes this all the way!
He adds to it a spiritual ingredient,
That softens our hearts to obey!

Murder, adultery, divorce, and swearing
Are attacked with an ironclad fist.
Revenge is only to be handled spiritually—
Love for others is at the top of the list!

Give to the needy, then prayer and fasting,
Are explained as only He can do.
There are rewards at the end of the rainbow,
AND worrying shouldn't be a part of you!

We can't judge others at all—
That's His job and His alone!
If we ask, seek, and knock,
We'll have blessings we've never known!

We are taught to go through life,
Taking the narrow path instead of the wide.
The narrow path is not crowded, but straight,
But the other is full of hatred and pride!

He speaks of bearing good fruit—
What a delight to bear good and not bad!
Let's be wise, in building our dwelling place,
And not foolish; it can end so bad!

These teachings we shall concentrate on,
And mold them into our daily living!
This "Sermon on the Mount", as it's called,
Is for His own to keep giving and giving!

It's Harvest Time

Here we are in winter,
The autumn time was long,
And God knows what we need,
Now, could my thoughts be wrong?

You see, God humors me,
He seems to know my desires—
I <u>needed</u> the autumn to be long—
Of its beauty, no one tires!

Besides, I'm still a farmer,
And the crops must still be in
Before cold or stormy weather
Comes first, then hard tell when!

The farmer suffers that loss,
It really stands to reason,
You can't get the loan paid, though,
By waiting for another season!

I found myself praising God
For each of those sunny days,
You've put off winter for me, God,
I'll forever sing your praise!

For, not only the yield is great,
But even the quality is high!
You continue to bless us, Lord,
As each lovely day goes by!

May we take time at harvest,
To bow and give thanks for it all.
Help us to take time to witness,
For, souls' harvest, too, is our call!

American Baptist Women's Ministries
2004

Five and one-half years at Wal-Mart

This particular time in my life,
Has been quite a blessing to me.
There have been many ups and down,
But that's part of life, you see!

The management is down-to-earth people,
They seem never to compel you.
They stock the shelves, even sweep the floor,
They tend to show you how, not just tell you!

My fellow associates are true friends,
They will always be whom I will praise.
Each one has lifted me so noticeably,
Were an inspiration for any bad days!

The people greeters were cooperative
In switching the schedule to comply
With family, church, and social life—
Sometimes, didn't even ask why!

The stockmen treated me like their grandma—
Were willing to do what I wanted done,
Whether stocking the ledge or getting carts—
Were so obliging and seemed to have fun!

The carts aren't new anymore,
The customers remind me of that.
I always say they're guaranteed to please,
As I lay out the welcome mat!

It was always a challenge for me
To keep up with locations of displays.
For, daily I was questioned by customers
To find items they'd needed for days!

The number of returns is overwhelming—
The public takes advantage of the system
Of bringing back items, old, worn out, or broken—
There are so many, I could never list 'em!

I've worked so close to the snack bar
And watched associates come and go.
We can always depend on **Mary**,
She's been good for me to know!

I'm so opposed to raffling—
Selling tickets at the door.
I've felt this sense of gambling
Is not what Wal-Mart stands for!

Customers shy away from us
When they see us asking for money.
I want them to feel glad they came.
I enjoy an atmosphere that's sunny!

The children at Riley Hospital
Need our support and attention,
I'm convinced if donations were given,
Our approach is with loving intention.

I owe to Wal-Mart a vote of thanks
For the privilege to work with my Master.
I've been blest to listen to the hurting world,
To ignore them would be a disaster!

For it's been a great chance to witness
To someone who needs a kind word.
If I speak with a Christlike attitude,
It may be all some have ever heard.

I've seen many well kept children,
Then I've seen many who are abused.
I've wanted to hug and love them,
But, you see, then I'd be accused!

Max and I want to travel
And see the world while we can.
Dedication and faithfulness to Wal-Mart
Can't be a part of the plan.

I plan to sit at the computer
And put together poems I've written.
A book of poetry is my goal—
It will take a lot of sittin'!

Wal-Mart will always be
My favorite place to shop.
I'll probably spend more time there,
The desire will never stop!

It is my prayer for Wal-Mart—
For associates and customers, too,
That we'll continue to work together
As God planned for us to do!

May Wal-Mart remain at the top
In community and civic affairs, too.
May sales keep growing as before—
I want God's best for all of you!

September, 1998

The following is a poem created to entice people to work with me in the **Amway (Quixtar)** business in 1989. It's called "**Sharing the Plan**". This approach was easier for me when acting as a motivator with one on one or with an audience.

I'd like to center my discussion right now
On four values important to many,
So sit back, relax, and please listen—
I won't make you uncomfortable, any!

First is money—dollars—cash!
It ranks high on the chart.
It's mankind's medium of exchange—
We'll work hard for it—and smart!

Time is so very valuable,
And we've all been allotted the same,
But use it right in duplication—
That's the name of the game!

Security, we shall consider—
It's on everybody's mind.—
Take care of it with this,
For it's the only one of its kind.

Maybe you have all you need,
And should you make a little more,
You can reach out and help someone,
It's what all God's people are for.

The "dream" is the drive that promotes action—
It's a goal you must set really high,
Now if money was no object,
What in the world would you buy?

If it's your desire to travel,
Where in the world would you go?—
Would you relax on beach after beach,
Or view God's creation really slow?

Is there something you'd like to stop doing?
Is there something you'd really like to do?
Aside from your family, would you help someone?—
There's a charity list, long—not a few!

According to "US News & World Report",
Here's some statistics to realize.—
It shows incomes versus lifestyles—
I think you're in for a surprise!

(In 1980 you made $10,000—one income, one life style, in 1990, you
earned $22,400 with two incomes and one life style, in 2000, you earned
$56,000 with three incomes and one life style.)

For an average working person,
Let's talk about the plan
Of working forty-five years
Just as hard as you can!

You work on the average
Of eight hours a day—
One hundred thousand hours total—
By then you're old and gray!—

You've worked all that time,
Taking good care of your wife,
Then you'll get $450 a month
For the rest of your life.

With this new plan I'm sharing—
You work from two to five years,
Just eight to ten hours weekly,
Unless you want to shift gears,

And put in extra time—
It's all up to you.
You can hurry or go slow,
Whatever you want to do!

A man named J. Paul Getty,
Who's a noted financier,
Says there are three ways to make money,
I shall show you right here!

Number one, there's investing,
But there're three facts you must know—
You must have money to begin,
And then wait for it to grow.

Yes, there's that time involved,
So it's not instant cash,
And it's quite a risk;
Yes, the market might crash!

Trading hours for dollars
Is money-maker number two.
According to Mr. Getty,
It's the way most people do.

Another word for that
Is a position or job.
We seem to have no other choice,
But go along with the mob.

Here's some statistics
Again from Mr. Getty,
After making lots of money,
It seems to fly like confetti!

(In '85 you made $50,000, kept
$38,000, in '95 you made $100,000,
kept $39,000, in '05 you made ?, kept ?)

Here's Mr. Getty's third way—
It's the simplest we need—
It's called "duplication",
It's most likely to succeed.

We must work hard and work smart,
We must follow those who lead.
If we follow directions,
We'll get it done in great speed!

McDonald's is a good example,
Of a business that's duplicated—
One goes up every seventeen hours,
Think what Ray Kroc has created!

But it takes a half million dollars
To start one of your own;
Sale of franchising has stopped,
Is what we've recently known.

These reports also tell us
Some big figures that keep rising—
Americans spend to the total of
Eighty-one billion dollars in advertising.

And as you go shopping for bargains,
Let me share with you this hint,
Each product has a mark-up
Of as much as seventy or eighty percent.

The trend now is "at home" shopping,
$171 billion dollars a year is done—
This fact leads me right into
The greatest system under the sun!

Network marketing is the name
Of this duplicating business—
Learning one step at a time,
To refrain from any dizziness.

Forty-eight percent of all millionaires
Are networking of this sort—
(These words are by John Sustina
And "US News & World Report".)

First, we are equipped with a clearing house,
Controlled by a company, debt-free—
Working with the Internet Support System,
Operating hand-in-hand, we shall see.

Over one thousand commonly known companies
Offer over 10,000 products, the best,
Cars, travel, clothes, furniture, insurance—
Takes hours to tell all the rest.

The bulk of this business is
Moving products we use every day—
Kitchen, bathroom, and personal supplies—
Consumables, needless to say.

Since there's no retail cost involved,
We pay in the 30% column.
Besides the savings there, you get
Money paid to you according to volume.

The system is set up with point value,
With one point with every $2 used.
One family will consume each month
Around $200—don't be confused,

See, 30% of $200
Is $60 saved—no tricks,
And a bonus for your performance—
Total saved and earned—66.

Doing just that much, it's worth it,
Saving 800 to $1,000 a year,
But sharing this system with six other people
Is a money-maker, wait 'til you hear!

The way to explain the income
Is to draw circles for each one involved.
If you get in the winner's circle,
Your cash problems soon will be solved.

Now, you and your six people
Will create the 1400 BV,
And then, 9% of that much cash
Is $126, you see!

Now, you must pay your six smart people
The 3% they're entitled to,
Leaving you $150
Saved and earned by you!

It gets much more exciting
As we use the 6-4-2 plan,
Encouraging the 6 to share with 4, and each
4 with 2, duplicating again and again!

The next level has 31 involved,
That figures $6200 in buying,
We're in the 18% bracket now,
Making over $1100, no denying!

Pay immediate 6 their earnings,
Which is $360 altogether—
You keep your savings and earnings—
It's over 750 in all kinds of weather!

Each of 4 shares with 2 now,
Building your number to 79—
That's $15,800—
Reaching the very top line!

Twenty-five % of that figure
Is three thousand nine hundred fifty,
Keeping 2,138 for your very own
Is really an income quite nifty!

You're now a direct distributor—
Meaning that products come to you,
Instead of traveling upline,
Like smaller pin-levels do.

Let's say you become direct,
And as you've shared this with more,
And one you've sponsored follows you,
Reaching that same top score—

It's called "breaking a direct",
And that creates an income, too.
For they will get their 2,000 a month—
For two generations, cash comes to you!

There are twenty-nine levels of income—
You learn their origin as you go,
Number one is buying the products,
A savings which can grow and grow.

Number two is income from sponsorship,
Number three is retirement, called ERI.
From 4 to 7 are bonuses,
Explain them—I don't even try!

The 8th level of income is this—
$100,000 a year, or so—
On to 29—it's phenomenal,
It just never ceases to grow!

So get a kit, application, and products,
From Amway, the company debt-free,
Get in business for yourself—
If you think you can't, ask me!

I can't answer all the questions,
But I go upline to find out who knows,
For it's a people-helping-people business,
It's unbelievable, then, how it grows!

You'll get tapes to keep you motivated,
Reading books is what directs have done.
You'll attend seminars and rallies—
They're tax-deductible and they're fun!

Number four is using the products—
Use the best—get cash in return,
Number five is simply STP—
Share the Plan—it's easy to learn.

Yes, these are the five steps to this business,
To reach the goal of your dreams,
Duplicating the successful ones—
It's not as hard as it seems!

Now you don't have to write poetry—
You share the plan your own way.
Just explain it how you understood it.
There're not any exact words to say!

However, if you want my poem,
Just ask and I'll share it with you.
There's a Xerox machine in the business—
Make you a copy, is what I'll do!

Think of those who need money.
To start, list one hundred people you know.
Fifty will say they'll meet with you,
But only ten will show!

Out of ten, five will admit,
They could use some extra dough.
You'll sponsor two or three of them.—
Yes, that figure seems low,

But, you're off and running, look up,
Set up another meeting,
Duplicate the first night strategy,
A few you'll be repeating!

At first, I wasn't excited,
But that feeling didn't last long,
I felt it was all impossible—
Got in—Man, was I wrong!

Amway Sponsors

Sharon and **Bob Dillman** are my sponsors.—
They're the best you'll find.—
The **Rude**s, my direct, are super—
Just keep that in mind!

Showleys are profit-sharing,
And they're super, too.—
So outreaching and helpful—
Good counselors for our crew.

My diamonds are special—
Keeping me on the right line.—
The greatest, and I love them—
They're **Tim** and **Cindy Kline**!

My down-line is my life-line—
Buying products galore.
And as we all buy our own products,
We will reach that high score!

All my children
Are in this system for me.
I praise God for them.—
I'm as pleased as I can be!

The Lord is blessing us,
As we all do our part.—
Yes, it's people helping people—
Seems to be straight from each heart!

I am the Dairy Queen—
Milking cows makes me strong—
I'll continue for a while—
But, believe me, not for long!

I enjoy writing poetry.
I like to make words rhyme.
So I do lots of thinking,
But can't do it every _____.
So all of us together here,
Can surely get it done.
I'll think up most of the words;
You'll come up with just _____.
Let's write about school,
This will be about the first day.
First we get out of bed,
And get on our knees to _____.
We must seek for God's presence,
As we head off to school.
We want Him to help us
To live the Golden _____.
Get to the breakfast table,
And eat a good meal.
The more we eat right,
The better we _____.
We bow our head
And thank God for it.
I can't pour the milk,
Maybe Mom will _____.
We put our clothes on,
We try to dress for the weather,
Then go catch the school bus,
So, we hold hands and stick _____.
We arrive at school,
Meet old friends, some new,
Go to our classroom—
That's what we should _____.

We listen to our teacher.
She always knows what's best.
We think hard for right answers,
When she gives us all a _____.
It's finally time for lunch.
Sometimes it's hard to wait.
I've always been instructed
To eat all that's on my _____.
When we go out for recess,
We'll play games and have fun.
It's usually quite a challenge
To see how fast we can _____.
The afternoon is long
For we're not used to school.
However, the new things we learn
Are really quite _____.
We get on the bus
To go home to Mom and Dad.
Now, you see, that first day of school
Really wasn't so _____.
"What's for supper?"
Is what we'll probably say,
"Oh, you must do your chores."
That's the price we gotta _____.
Then homework, if there's any,
We must keep it up, and not fail.
We could get into trouble;
We could land in _____.
Oh, no, not in this country—
Punishment is not that severe,
But we want a good education
To help save this nation we hold _____.

It's night time and bed time;
Time to get back on our knees,
And praise God for the goodness.
God gives blessings when we say _____.
Thanks for your help,
The right words come faster,
When we put our minds together,
It's not quite such a _____.
We can turn to our Bibles
And read Romans 8:28;
Take seriously what it says,
We will enter Heaven's _____.

Section 9.
Bible School and Salvation

This section is small, but mighty.

...for there will be a time for every activity, a time for every deed. Ecclesiastes 3:17a

Sow for yourselves righteousness, reap the fruit of unfailing love, and break up your unplowed ground; for it is TIME to seek the Lord. Hosea 10:12

Bible School—1998, Mexico Baptist Church

Now, it's become sharing time
To tell others of our blessing.
What I have to share with you,
May not be what you're guessing.

I'm getting older and set in my ways—
Wasn't in favor of the literature or the plan—
My thoughts for saving children,
Was to teach them all you can.—

Not with the outer space rockets
And robots that came with the lesson,
But with scripture and nothing foolish—
I was wrong, I must be confessin'!

For to be "kind" and "helpful" and "thankful"
Were crammed in every minute.—
They responded so lovingly and graciously,
I am thankful I got to be in it!

Teresa and her crew had the music.
As you've heard, it was very well done.
She can come up with the music,
Better than anyone under the sun!

Ann and **Barb** were leaders in the nursery,
They had a lively group, like 12 or 13—
These ladies have the patience of Job, himself—
More than anyone you've ever seen!

With **Donna** and **Dick** through the tunnel,
Bible stories we did explore.—
The children will never forget that,
They waited around, wishing for more!

Steve, **Tom**, and **Lisa** were phenomenal,
Providing games and recreation that fit—
Right along with the theme for each night—
How more co-operative can you "git"?

Gina and **Debbie** controlled refreshments,
Each evening kept getting more exciting.
Food was chosen and prepared
Along with themes—all so inviting!

Eva was quiet, but yet bold, there
In teaching reverence and thankfulness, too.
The young responded to her teaching,
Just like they were supposed to do!

Bev was our suffering little robot,
Her sacrifice was most successful, bar none;
She hinted what we'd be learning each evening.
The crafts made were so unique and fun!

Pastor and **Eileen**'s wedding anniversary
Was celebrated with a cake and a song.
Years of a good life together,
Enjoying them together wasn't wrong!

You see, they have shared their leadership,
With qualities that lead us to the Master.
Children have a tendency to follow,
If convincing words come from the pastor!

We had many helpers each night,
I don't want to leave out any—
A blast-off to these good people,
It's difficult to say how many!

All were generous in giving
To needy kids overseas,
By bringing lots of school supplies
To those who are NOT hard to please!

All of the young people were phenomenal
In their response to discipline and behavior.
It is our prayer from times being together,
Will cause one to come to the Savior!

There was lots of hard work and dedication
In preparing for these events to recall—
But if just one soul will come to Christ,
It was well worth it all!

Mark 10:14   Jesus said to them, "Let the little children come to me, and do not hinder them, for the kingdom of God belongs to such as these."

Helpers: **Mary Beth, Mary Ruth, Emily, Greg, Linda, Shad, Trisha, Bob, Peg, Jack, Michele, Ann, and Marie**

**Promotions to next class—Sunday School—
Jeremiah**—This certificate is for you—
You're not tiny any more!
You'll have a different teacher,
To explain what the Bible is for!

Congratulations, **Ashley,**
Your mother won't be your teacher,
She'll be right around the corner, though,
In case you need to reach her!

Congratulations, **Whitney,**
You've advanced to the next class!
I know Jesus is smiling,
He really wanted you to pass!

Congratulations, **Michael,**
You've been a pleasant little guy,
You're a good example
For us all to live by!

Mallory—Congratulations,
You'll be taught by **Jerry,**
You've a desire for musical talent—
How much do we enjoy it?—Very!

Ian, we're so proud of you;
When we're singing, you sing out!
May the Lord bless your efforts
In church, school, or out and about!

Congratulations, **Spencer,**
You seem to have good training
To get your work done or wait for
Instructions—
A crown from Jesus you are gaining!

Congratulations to you, **Rebecca,**
We are pleased to have you,
Your beauty and eagerness is noticed
In all that you try to do!

Carlie, congratulations to you—
You have proved to us you're aware
That Bible School and Sunday School are
Valuable, and we know you care!

Congratulations are for you, **Chelsey,**
You, too, advance one more step.
Your loving smile and happy face
Makes us adults have a lot more pep!

Ashley is to be congratulated,
You seem shy, but work with speed
To help us all shine for Jesus!—
You are just who we need!

Congratulations and best wishes to you,
As you move on up, **Grace.**
Your Christlikeness and sweet attitude,
Just shows all over the place!

Deb and **John**—To you who have completed
The task you set out to do—
We give you honor and a million times, thanks—
May God pour out blessings on you!

To those in continuing service,
In the areas needing love and persistence,
You've been there with a prayer on your lips,
Making sure missions stay in existence!
We give praise and thanks to you!

Hands

Hands that are busy and useful,
May sort of get worn out and rough,
But why keep our hands tender,
For our fellow man, we can't do enough.

We are thankful for our hands, O God,
Thankful for energy to use them,
If we've been approached by those in need,
It's our prayer, we'll not refuse them!

So we think of the hands least talked of,
The mission machine that prayer often runs,
The hands that cause miracles to happen—
The "Praying Hands"—they are the ones!

"MARRIAGE"
by Nina Lynch

A timely issue has come up
Regarding marriage of man and wife.
Our nation is under great attack,
As to how to plan each life.

As we reach time for marriage,
Is it not the thing to do?—
Search the scriptures for guidance—
God's explanation is not new!

For in Matthew and Corinthians we find,
Man to man and woman to woman isn't His plan!
Marriage is man wed to woman,
And woman is to be wed to man!

Prayer

What's a good definition,
Of a prayer I might send?
Is it conversing with God,
Like I would with another friend?

To pray without ceasing,
In the scripture we are told.
We pray when we are young;
We pray when we are old.

How can we pray constantly,
When we are so busy?
For work gets piled up,
Until we are dizzy!

I've heard it said,
I know you have, too,
"When we're too busy to pray,
We're too busy!" How true!

To pray is a privilege,
God gave to everyone;
There's not a better use for time,
Anywhere under the sun!

We should pray for each other,
Lifting those up to Him,
Who may need healing
Or in trouble to the brim!

I know God keeps secrets,
I can tell Him anything,
I know He will listen,
He treats me like a King!

We should have prayers of thanks,
For many a material blessing,
We take so much for granted,
We should be confessing.

Prayer is a tool
For us carpenters to use,
Helping build God's kingdom,
Not one soul can we lose!

When we go to battle,
Having Satan to defeat,
Let's use our prayer weapon
On the enemy we meet!

I praise God for opportunities
To witness with prayer;
I can always count on
His presence to be there!

Let's not fail to remember
God hears us when we pray.
He may say "yes", He may say "No",
We must follow Him anyway!

Salvation

Salvation for you is my concern—
May I share what the scriptures say?
Starting with Romans 3:23,—
It's easy to explain it this way!

You see, "all have sinned and fallen short
Of the glory of God"—and that means
None of us are perfect in the sight of God—
Children? older ones? even teens!

Then in Romans 5:8 we learn
That God demonstrates His love for us all,
In that, while we were still sinners,
He sent us His Son, so we'd not fall!

In John 3:15, we learn,
That all who believe God's Son
May have eternal life,
And it's through Jesus, the only One!

John 3:18 talks of condemnation,
The condemned are those with a spiritual need!
You must believe in God's only Son—
If you do, you've salvation indeed!

Romans 6:23 talks about wages—
Yes, the wages of sin is death—
You'll want to have eternal life,
Before you take one more breath!

So confess with your mouth
And believe in your heart,
That God raised Jesus from the dead.
He tells in His Word of this great gift—
You just need to believe what He said!

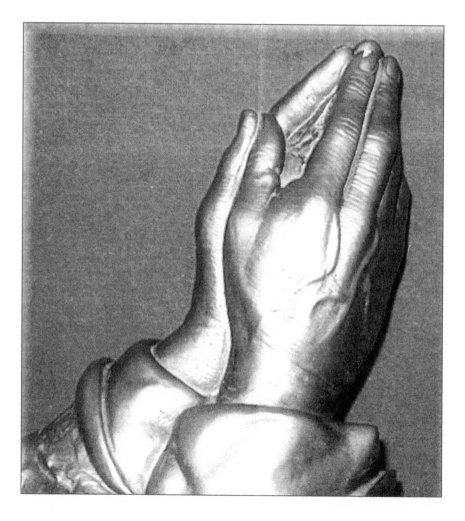

(DO YOU? If YES, then,)

Salvation now is yours—
Isn't that great?

You've accepted and
Believed what you should!
Now a new life is yours in Jesus—
He wants you to share it, if you would!

*Psalm 68:19   What a glorious Lord; He who daily bears our burdens also
gives us our salvation.*

About the Author

First time author, Nina A. Lynch, was born in Bethlehem Township of Cass County, on a farm near Twelve Mile, Indiana. She was the seventh of nine children, born to Russell and Goldie Coffing. She graduated from Metea High School. She was cashier at The S. S. Kresge Company in Logansport for three years. She married Raymond Warner, who was a dairy farmer in Miami County. They had four children—Nancy, Greg, Leah, and Hal. She enjoyed working with the dairy, and counted it a blessing and a challenge. She enjoyed working in the music department of the Baptist Church at Perrysburg, mostly with children and young people, playing both piano and organ—(not at the same time!). She became involved with this same type of ministry at the Mexico Baptist Church as well as in the missions ministry of The American Baptist Women. She saw the need to create devotional type material to be used in this area. The Indiana Extension Homemakers Association plays an important part in her life and she has been a member of that organization for over fifty years. Her husband, Raymond, passed away suddenly in 1983, and after struggling with the dairy for thirteen years, she married her high school sweetheart, who had become a widower. She and Max began a new life in Rochester, where she was a people greeter at Wal-Mart. Max has been an encourager to help her pursue the art of writing words, thoughts, and happenings of life and reach a goal of her dreams—publishing a book of poetry. She was an associate for Amway (Quixtar) products, where she met many friends, too, who promote peace and goodwill, and press on to that goal. She tried to keep all of her poems she has written in a place, to compile them some day, in a book to share. After all of these years, don't you think—"it's about time"?

Made in the USA
Monee, IL
29 September 2022